DEAD RECKONING

Experiences of a World War II Fighter Pilot

BY

ALAN K. ABNER

BURD STREET PRESS

A Division of White Mane Publishing Company

All photographs not otherwise credited are from the author's collection.

This Burd Street Press book
was printed by
Beidel Printing House, Inc.
63 West Burd Street
Shippensburg, PA 17257 USA

In respect for the scholarship contained herein, the acid-free paper used in this book meets the guidelines for permanence and durability of the Committee on Production Guidelines for Book Longevity of the Council on Library Resources.

For a complete list of available publications
please write
Burd Street Press
Division of White Mane Publishing Company, Inc.
P. O. 152
Shippensburg, PA 17257 USA

Library of Congress Cataloging-in Publication Data

Abner, Alan K., 1921-
    Dead reckoning : experiences of a World War II fighter pilot / by
Alan K. Abner.
        p.   cm.
    ISBN 1-57249-025-X
    1. Abner, Alan K., 1921-   . 2. World War, 1939-1945--Aerial
operations, American. 3. United States. Army Air Forces. Fighter
Group, 357th--History. 4. United States. Army Air Forces-
-Biography. 5. World War, 1939-1945--Personal narratives, American.
6. Fighter pilots--United States--Biography. I. Title.
F790.A66 1997
940.54 4973--DC21   96-48748
                                                              CIP

PRINTED IN THE UNITED STATES OF AMERICA

Dedicated to
Major Don Bochkay
squadron commander

TABLE OF CONTENTS

PREFACE

World War II fighter planes were more akin to the Spads and Fokkers of the First World War than they were to today's combat jets. Eddie Rickenbacker and the Red Baron could immediately relate to the likes of Gentile, Bong, and Yeager. World War II fighter pilots in all branches of service, Army, Marines, and Navy, in Europe and the Pacific theaters still flew "by the seat of their pants." Combat quickly became a one-on-one deadly duel. After the battle was over and the various squadron elements were scattered widely over enemy terrain, the fighter pilots then became navigators. Each pilot had to traverse the 500 or so miles back to home base, surely to be diverted only by possible enemy aircraft encounters, or to escort a struggling, defenseless allied bomber home to friendly territory. *Dead Reckoning* describes how it was in the cockpit of a Mustang fighter plane as a member of the 357th Fighter Group which scored a record 56 victories on January 14, 1945.

"Dead Reckoning" is an aviation term that describes the navigation technique used in flying an aerial course relying on visual landmarks. "Dead Reckoning" is a double entendre of the term which describes the ultimate decisions made by an Oregon farm youth, influenced by months of intensive training and 50 missions of combat over Europe in 1944 and 1945. These decisions demonstrate vividly how a cow hand can become a professional fighter pilot.

"The Yoxford Boys"

IN MEMORIAM TO THE FIGHTER PILOTS
WHO MADE THE SUPREME SACRIFICE IN
AIR BATTLES OVER EUROPE AND IN HONOR

OF THOSE WHO SERVED IN THE

357TH FIGHTER GROUP
362ND 363RD 364TH FIGHTER SQUADRONS
AND ALL SUPPORT UNITS.

LEISTON, ENGLAND
1944 - 1945

688 1/2 ENEMY AIRCRAFT DESTROYED
THEY FULFILLED THEIR MISSION

Our Plaque at the USAF Academy Cemetery Memorial Wall

CHAPTER 1 *AN OREGON TRAIL TO BERLIN*

"Come to America. 'Tis truly a land of opportunity," the letter said. "All you have to do is carry a hod full of bricks up a twelve story building, and there's a fella up there that does all of the work!"

My dad loved to tell that story about his early ancestor, the first Abner to come to America at the turn of the 19th century. Three generations later, the Welsh immigrant's great-grandson, John Abner, my paternal grandad, was a practicing physician in Hamlet, Indiana, and the medical line stopped there. Doc Abner's son, Warren LeRoy, my dad, though pressed to follow in his father's footsteps, compromised and graduated from Valpariso University in pharmacy, and thereafter, never rolled a pill. Young Roy stashed his diploma in a trunk in the family attic, and "rode the rails" underneath boxcars and headed west to become a rancher.

My maternal grandmother and her Episcopalian family came West with a Mormon wagontrain in 1840, and settled in Ogden, Utah. It was there she met and married Albert Bowler, a Canadian immigrant of Irish descent. Bowler Sr. was a blacksmith-inventor, debater, raconteur and a genial man with a thirst for convivial spirits. My grandparents, this odd couple, the high-church Episcopalian and the Orangeman, had three sons, and two daughters. Sylvia with her eldest brother, Bert, were the only ones of the brood to graduate from college. My mother earned her teacher's certificate at Washington State College at Pullman, and was a country schoolmarm when she met and married my dad in Lewiston, Idaho in 1906. Sylvia and Roy had four sons. Francis Burr was the eldest, Donald Adair next, Paul LaRoy, and nine years after the others, me.

1

My father's married career up until the time of my arrival had been involved first in farming for the first ten or so years. Then, being exempt in World War I as a farmer and family man, he was active in a Labor Employment Agency with his brothers-in-law. Post war, he became a partner in a successful chain of men's clothing stores that lasted until the Crash of '29. Finally, at long last, he managed to return to his first love, ranching, and the spread he acquired in Newberg, Oregon was the scene of my most enjoyable childhood.

I came from a "broken home"; my mother was a Hoover Republican and my dad a New Deal Democrat. Sylvia saw to it that her four sons were baptized in the Episcopal church, and I was trotted off to Sunday School weekly until I got old enough to play hooky. Dad, a Mason, did not go to church except for wakes and weddings. Though he did admit to me one time when I questioned some religious practice, that "Bob Ingersoll was the most famous atheist in America. Yet, on his death bed, asked for a priest." That summed up dad's beliefs nicely.

Our family was one of almost perfect harmony. The boys never fought each other, and except for rather heated political arguments, no one ever went to sleep with unsettled disagreements. My dad never ordered me to do anything...he asked. Mom spanked me regularly, usually for running off to explore the countryside, but never with enough vigor to call it a beating. Discipline wasn't something talked about. It was something self imposed by wanting to be loved by your parents and your brothers; not be a "fool kid."

Roy Abner was a "scientific" farmer, due perhaps to his early college training. Luther Burbank was his "mentor," and the Oregon Agricultural College agent was a personal friend. He gloried in developing hybrid berry growths and grafted fruit trees. He bred and maintained a fine herd of registered, purebred Jersey dairy animals, and was readily available for testing range grasses and novel irrigation projects. Though advanced in agricultural matters, other modern innovations, except for the radio, didn't hold much interest for him. Though he was an adequate carpenter, he wasn't good with engines. Most mechanical things were a mystery.

But he "talked" animal language. He could calm a skittish horse with some kind of mysterious mutterings; a wild-as-a-deer heifer would behave for him. Dogs, cats and even mother pigs welcomed his ear scratchings. He had great patience with animals, but very little tolerance for abusive people.

I don't know how much of one's character is inherited...but I sure believe in a happy, healthy home environment.

Albert Bowler was 16 years old when he took his ancestor's advice and left Canada for the States. He did indeed carry bricks. He did all kinds of hard manual labor in eastern cities at first, until he finally made his way west, and learned to be a cowboy. From Texas to Wyoming he worked cattle, finally putting together enough of a stake to set out a homestead in the Orgeon country. It was here that he prospered, married, and raised a family. He had never visited the Old Country. It would be me, his grandson, who would make that long trip across the ocean.

"If man was meant to fly, God would have given him wings." This wasn't an original thought expressed by the elder Bowler. He'd heard it said when Orville and Wilbur Wright made their first flight, and even though airplanes could now be seen daily, flying over their ranch at Oregon, he still viewed them with some skepticism. He no longer used the expression, especially since Pearl Harbor, where the Japanese had destroyed the American fleet with flying machines. "Airplanes were probably here to stay, but he sure as hell wasn't going to get in one. No sir!"

Roy Abner, Grandad Bowler's son-in-law, never said, "he wouldn't get in one." He just hadn't gotten around to it. Once, during the Depression, he had worked at road building with the W.P.A. (Works Progress Administration) to help keep the ranch from going under. He'd even learned to drive a road scraper, but that was the biggest and most complicated piece of machinery he ever ran. The combine he and other ranchers shared at harvest time was operated by a "custom crew," and he was secretly glad he didn't have to worry about operating it. A pickup truck, a Ford tractor, and the family sedan he could handle, and there wasn't a horse within 20 miles he couldn't ride. But Roy Abner did not leave any apparent tradition or keen interest in aviation that could possibly influence the next generation.

There were early signs that I was "maybe a little fey," as my Grandad Bowler described it. It was true that even as a small child I seemed to have an insatiable curiosity about almost everything that moved. The fish and minnows that swam just under the surface of Chehalem Creek that ran through our property created a shaded fairyland. I spent hours sailing small boats made of bark and sticks through the ripples and the shallows. But my most intense fascination was with things that flew. The whirring of a covey of quail exploding out of the grass almost under foot was enough to give you a start. A hummingbird hovering over a succulent blossom seemed to do the impossible easily, and butterflies were a never ending delight. I was stunned, almost indignant when one of my visiting town chums suggested I start a collection of these beautiful creatures. To catch and kill one, and impale it on a board, or press it under a glass was unthinkable. "Boy, what a dumb thing to do," was my reaction. That town chum "was really stupid, and might as well be from another planet."

Of course, life on a working ranch resulted in a certain number of living things that were destined to die. "Some critters are born so a man can live," was the way my grandad put it. I soon learned that you never named a calf. Calves and young piglets were called meat. Even chickens were culled; the young roosters became fryers, and the pullets were saved for layers. When the layers ceased to produce eggs, they appeared on the Sunday table as a roast. I finally decided this was all just something you didn't think about. "That's the way it is."

One summer morning when I was nine years old, my mother came out on the front porch of our ranch house to shake the crumbs from a table cloth, just in time to see me on the roof of the big barn, taking off with a pair of wings attached to my arms with sack strings. I'd fashioned my "airplane" out of a big cardboard carton. Luckily, I landed on a manure pile and wasn't hurt. Then! When Dad rode in later and learned of my solo flight, it was a quick trip to the machine shed, and a hardy helping of razor strap applied to the seat of this pilot's pants. The only other time my dad had licked me was for smoking corn silk. That time, the strap had cured my "nicotine habit" instantly. But this time it did not curb my fascination with flying.

Why is it that a "ranch" is more impressive than a "farm"? A "farm" conjures up visions that include a big hip roof barn, usually red, a long, low white-washed chicken house with rotating ventilators on the roof, and a square two-storied house with no redeeming architectural features. The land surrounding the buildings is usually flat, and always under cultivation. A few big elm trees shade the dwelling, and nearby a small orchard of apple, pear and cherry trees, and in the right climate, a peach or apricot may be found. It's a peaceful enough setting in the Grant Wood tradition, but it's dull.

Now a "ranch" is something else. Oh, there's a barn, but no one gives it much thought or attention and it's never been painted. The roof was shingled originally, but through the years it's had its various holes and gaps repaired with sheets of corrugated tin here and there so it more resembles a tattered patchwork metal quilt. At one time it was used to store loose hay, but when hay balers came in, the bales were stacked alongside and covered with huge tarps. So much for sleeping in the haymow.

I was pretty sure that we lived on a "ranch." Our barn had never been painted and the 40-acre alfalfa field that stretched out in front of the house towards town was the only level piece of ground on the place. Over a hundred acres of the ranch was in pasture. A creek that in Texas would be called a river, ran the full length of the property, winding along through tree-shaded banks and was highlighted by a swimming hole that was 60 yards wide, 150 yards long and 8 feet in depth at its deepest point. The spread was perfectly laid out for a golf course, but at this time the only players were calves.

To be a "barefoot boy with cheeks of tan" in Oregon's Chehalem Valley in the '30s was the best of all worlds to grow up in. Play was something you did when grown-up work and chores were done. And play was with things you invented to do alone. Gadgets from a toy store or sporting goods shop were almost unknown. Model airplanes were good. Not the kind that actually flew, but heavier ones that started with a piece of 2 x 4 and ended up whittled and planed into a semblance of a Spad or Fokker. Basketball shooting was done by tossing an old kitten-ball through a barrel hoop nailed to the barn. Boomerangs that never came back ended up in the brush down the hill by the creek. Kite remnants clung to the topmost branches of the huge hungry elms that shaded the house. The only recreational devices that endured were an old steel fly rod that Grandad Pat had wielded for some 30 years and a .22 single shot Winchester rifle with a real silver-tipped front sight.

I didn't have the patience my dad had for fly fishing, but I did become the deadly enemy of the gray digger squirrels that ravaged the pasture land with holes that could break the leg of a gamboling heifer or a running horse. I didn't care much for the killing part of it. But I was secretly proud of being known as a sure shot.

Daily chores were numerous. Cows to milk before daylight and after dark. Chickens to feed, wood to be chopped and brought into the woodbox; all provided a warm-up for the real work of the day.

Haying, cultivating, irrigating were a kind of fun. After all, it was man's work, and sweating with the adults in the family was a way of hurrying the growing-up process. Of course, "the kid" on the crew started out as a gopher; go-fer this and go-fer that. It really was a necessary chore and one that didn't waste the time of a real hand who then wasn't distracted from doing a job by having to run and fetch something in the middle of things. It wasn't quite man's work, but it was the next thing to it.

At 15 years old, I was too tall and too skinny to pass for a boxer. I stood at five feet nine inches and weighed 148 pounds soaking wet. My hair was flaming red, and anyone calling me "Brick" or "Carrot top" was in for a scrap. I'd only had few bare-knuckled fights growing up, but somehow I had won. Anyone watching at that time would have said I outlasted rather than outfought my opponent. It wasn't that I wasn't a pretty good athlete and physically well coordinated. It was just because of my slow-to-burn temper. As I grew into my teens, it took a lot to get me riled, but when I'd had enough, I did not try to out-box my challenger. I flat went out to destroy him! I did observe some rules; I didn't bite; and I didn't kick a man who was down. And when the foe was beaten, I didn't punish him further. All of this "sportsmanship" would have turned my grandad cold. His theory was, "You had to bust a couple of their ribs. Layin' up in bed for a couple of weeks gave 'em time and a chance to ponder on their mistake."

When Don Abner, my older brother, came home from college after his freshman year, he announced that he'd made the varsity boxing team, and hadn't lost a match.

I was delighted, proud and pleading, "Boy, that's great, Don. Now you can teach me. I saved up and bought two pairs of 16 ounce gloves, but the guys I know don't know anything about boxing, and it's no fun just bangin' away at each other. I want to know how to really box!"

He was more than willing to be my coach. I had already proved my athletic ability playing high school football and basketball, and there was no reason I couldn't be equally good in the ring. Besides, it would be great working out all summer with a "sparring partner," and it wouldn't hurt his chances of again making the University of Oregon boxing team in the fall.

The boxing coach at the University Don attended was an "old pro." In his youth he'd been the third ranked welterweight in the world as a professional. And he had the scars to prove it. He was a firm believer in the traditional fundamentals of this amateur sport, but once a student had fairly well mastered the ABCs, he embellished the art with some techniques usually found only in the ranks of those who boxed for a living. Don had been a quick study, and combined with considerable natural ability, he'd advanced rapidly. And, he was smart enough to teach what he knew.

My dad was used to the horseplay his sons had carried on while growing up, so he didn't pay too much attention to our latest game. But one evening, as he told it later, chores done, as he was leaving the barn, he heard some new sounds coming from behind the machine shed where we had set up our "training ring." Moving quietly, he edged closer, and from behind a tractor parked near the building, he had a ringside seat without our knowing he was anywhere near. He knew quite a bit about prize fighting and followed the exploits of Joe Louis, the "Brown Bomber," with considerable interest. He was surprised he said, that he watched these two contestants doing a pretty passable job of it.

Though I was the younger, I was the taller of the two of us. I had the reach advantage of a couple of inches on my brother and used the properly thrown left jab Don had taught me to good effect. Don, though two inches shorter, had a physique that would develop into a classic middleweight. He was very quick and easily slipped most of the jabs. It was not the intensity of the blows that bothered him. It was the size of those "16-ounce pillows" that obscured his vision, and I kept that left moving in.

My dad, watching his two sons closely, waited for the inevitable to happen. He had seen and engaged in friendly contests that started out as mild tests of strength or skill, then develop into more intense conflicts. It could happen here.

Don was in no danger of being outclassed by his younger brother. His strategy in this contest was primarily of a defensive nature. He easily blocked or slipped my left jab, and I, a younger novice, had yet to learn about right crosses and counterpunches. But I continued to thrust with that long left lead, and the law of averages finally was enforced.

Don, bored with blocking and slipping jabs, suddenly tried a body feint leading to a right hand counterpunch, and he missed.

Excited by the unexpected move, I lashed out with the hardest thrown left I had ever unleashed, and it caught Don flush on the nose.

Reacting instinctively, he countered with a wide left hook to my head, followed by a hard right hand to my midsection that doubled me up, and I dropped to one knee.

"Goddamn, Alan, I'm sorry! I didn't mean to hit you so hard," he cried. He quickly knelt by me and asked anxiously, "Are you hurt bad? God, I'm sorry."

"No. Hey, I'm O.K.," I said. Finally, I slowly raised and straightened up. I remember I looked at my older brother with an expression that was new to both of us; an astonishment that quickly faded to a sort of wonderment, then was replaced by a new kind of respect. "Boy," I said, "you can really go when you want, can't you? That was something else!"

The sparring match was over for that day. Stripping off the mitts, we both started arm in arm towards the house. Our father, who had witnessed the bout, and liked to tell about it, nearly sputtered aloud, disclosing his hiding place, when he heard me say with mock concern to my teacher, "By the way, your nose has almost stopped bleeding."

I never had another street fight. I never ran into a challenger who after a quiet close-up decided to press his initial impulse into taking me on. Just lucky, I guess. I did, however, continue to box through my high school years.

The local P.A.L. Club (Police Athletic League) welcomed "The Farmer," as they called me, into their ranks. I went 17 wins for 18 outings in the amateurs, and ended my career at 148 pounds in the Semi Finals of the Regional P.A.L. tournament in Portland.

As I've told anyone interested in the scar over my right eye, "That guy was built like an orangutan. He was at least three or four inches shorter than I was, and his arms were three or four inches longer than mine. In the first round, out of nowhere, he hit me in the right eye with a left hand, not exactly a hook, that came out of left field. I never saw it coming!"

I lasted through the first round, but in the second took two more slashing shots to my swollen right eye, and finally the round was stopped due to a now freely bleeding cut. I was never knocked down or out in my brief boxing career, but the cut that required a 16-stitch sew-up halted my pugilistic ambitions.

"He really put his brand on me," I would recall when relating the story of my last ring appearance. "Look at that scar," I would say, pointing to a spot over my right eye. "Notice, it's a perfect T. The guy's name was Titus."

She stood almost 17 hands and weighed about a ton.

"I really meant to get a good mule, but this old girl really caught my eye." My dad, for all of his 50 odd years was just a little embarrassed. He'd gone to the livestock auction that summer morning with the intention of buying a cultivator-horse. Or better yet, an older, gentle mule; one that wouldn't give "the kid" any problems handling the harnessing and hooking up to a row cultivator and working a garden of row crops or the corn patch that provided feed for the hogs and chickens. Mules, with their little, careful feet were by far the best for this kind of work. Luckily for Babe, a big gray Percheron mare, there were no mules on the dock that day, and Roy Abner knew a great horse when he saw one.

"Migod, look at the size of them feet," my brother Paul said, turning to gaze in wonderment at his father. "Why, they're bigger than a milk bucket. She'll be great for stompin' out grass fires."

Dad, disregarding his son's good-humored kidding, looked fondly at the huge, handsome animal. "When I was a lad, our neighbor had a pair of Clydesdales, both a lot bigger than her, and folks would come from miles around just to look at 'em. Why, they could pull down a church if they was asked to. And talk about dainty. They could tiptoe through a mine field and never trip a wire. Babe here isn't as big as them, but she'll also show you a thing or two you don't know about bein' a horse."

Up til now I had eyes only for the cow horses, the Morgans and quarter horses that my dad and the other hands rode handling beef stock, but suddenly I "took a shine," as my grandad put it, to the big, gentle mare.

Seeing his grandson's interest in the horse, Grandad Bowler took to doing a little research in the "cycle-pedee" as he called it.

"The Frenchies bred 'em back in the Middle Ages for the knights to ride as war horses. With all that armor and the like they wore, it took a stout creature to carry 'em. And their 'steed,' as they called 'em, still had to be sure-footed and quick to win the fights they got into. Those knights weren't too interested in a speed horse cause they weren't long on runnin' away."

Suddenly, "Alan's Horse," as she soon was known, became a source of great fantasies for a youthful, adventurous mind. A cultivator with very little alteration could quickly become a Roman chariot. And an occasional ride to the watering trough, with young "Galahad" perched on her broad back, became a solemn march in search of a dragon.

"You know, she trots real good when you coax her a little," I told my grandad, "and, have you noticed how she picks up her front feet when she does? Just like she was in a parade."

The old man, sure of the new found knowledge he had just picked up from the Cycle-Peedee, was quick to verify his grandson's observations.

"Course she's got a fancy gait when she's a mind to. That's why to this day she's 'bout the only horse a circus bare-back rider will have anything to do with. Without them Percherons it wouldn't be much of a show I can tell you."

A few short years later when I enlisted to embark on my own "Crusade," my last evening at the ranch was spent with my two Alsation shepherd dogs and my "Frenchie War Horse."

December 7, 1941. Pearl Harbor..."Date of Infamy." Everyone's life changed that Sunday afternoon when President Franklin Roosevelt's familiar voice came over the radio with the most electrifying announcement anyone had ever heard. In an instant, the plans, hopes, and aspirations of all Americans were altered in some way to fit this dramatically new situation that would change their lives for months and years to come. It was not different in Newberg, Oregon.

It was only a matter of hours until the rumors began to fly. Japanese submarines were said to have been seen off the coast of California. Up and down the Pacific Coast, air raids, sabotage, poisoned water reservoirs, incendiary fires; all rumored to have been instigated by the "Japs." Invasion, to some, seemed imminent.

Life on the Abner Ranch went on much as usual, though no one missed the early morning, noontime and evening radio newscasts. But, there were still chores to be done, and Sylvia Abner went determinedly ahead with the customary preparations for the coming family Christmas festivities. I spent a little more time than was my custom with classmates and friends. The topic that dominated our conversation was not surprisingly the war.

"And what might you be doin' with that deer rifle, me boy, it bein' out of huntin' season?" my grandad stood in the doorway of the machine shed looking down at me, seated on a milk stool, where I was busy cleaning and polishing an ancient 30-30 Winchester.

I paused in my ministrations to "Old Betsy," as we called the weapon, and looked up at him as he stood, unsmiling, gazing down at me waiting for my answer.

"Well, Grandad," I said. "Lee, Gerry and Kenny are coming out in a little while, and we're going to run down to the coast this afternoon. The county sheriff said last nite that he'd heard there were Japanese submarines lying off shore near Tillamook, and that they could be planning a landing on the beaches sometime tonite. He's taking his deputies and the posse down today, and we thought we'd better go along and help out."

There was a long silence as my grandad mulled over this latest war bulletin. He told me he recalled his own youth in Ireland, and similar alarms about the "Black and Tans," and the hysteria that followed those inflammatory reports. He had known fear, and had experienced violent death at first hand. But, he could also remember, he said, what it was like to be young and full of the fire of patriotism, and the willingness to take up arms to protect your country or your cause.

"I know how you feel, lad," said the old man. "It's hard to know what to believe and what to do when your courage is challenged. I don't know, however, as I'd rely too heavy on the word of that damned fool sheriff. He's mostly mouth, and I know he's never been shot at. He's not what one of these radio fellers would call a 'reliable source'."

This was one of the longest speeches I'd ever heard from my usually taciturn grandad. The very length of it showed how important it was to him. And what he said did make a lot of sense.

"Yeah. He is kind of a dude," I argued. "I wondered about that 10-gallon hat and those pearl-handled six guns he wore, until I saw him ride a horse in the 4th of July parade two years ago. Migod, Grandad, I didn't think that poor old swayback pinto was going to get that tub o'lard to the end of Main Street."

The old man grinned at the recollection of that day. "Yep. He cut quite a figure all right. Makes you wonder about a man who doesn't know what's so obvious to everyone else. He's not the kind of feller I want tellin' me when and who to shoot at."

The old crook-stem briar pipe came out of his faded blue jumper, and was filled and tamped with great care. Lighting up with a kitchen match, he stepped out into the slight drizzle that had begun to fall, and with a cloud of blue smoke now filling the air around him he made his final observation.

"If I was goin' to do any soldierin', I reckon I'd sign up with an outfit that knowed what it was doin'. And I'd try to do it right."

Well, I put the 30-30 back in the gun rack. I knew now what had been nagging at me since last night when today's plan had been formed by my three friends. "I was about to be made a fool of! Not by my pals; they meant well. But grandad was right. If you're going to war, you'd better sign up, and as he had said, do it right." My thoughts returned to an earlier conversation.

"I wonder if Dave was serious when he was talking about enlisting in the Army Air Corps?"

It was 26 miles on old U.S. 99W from Newberg to Portland. The appointment was for 10:00 o'clock, and we'd both gotten up before daylight to allow plenty of time to get there early. It wasn't every day that a guy enlisted in the U.S. Army Air Corps. And we didn't intend to be late for this first call to duty.

"Well, for one thing it sure beats hell out of sitting up to your butt in a fox hole full of rain water, or swimming around in the middle of the ocean spitting salt water. At least in the air corps, you're dry most of the time." These remarks, punctuated by the slapping of the windshield wipers, were expressed by me to my pal Dave Boss as we slowly drove through a typical "Oregon mist" towards that state's largest city.

"You got it," said Dave. "The only line I remember from English Lit. is 'Water, Water, everywhere.' No wonder we're known as 'Webfeet.' At least the flying schools in the air corps are in Texas, Arizona and California. That alone is a good enough reason to join up with an outfit that has sense enough to train where the weather's good."

This apparent obsession with rain and weather by both of us was not peculiar just with us. We had both been born and raised as Oregonians, and had worked in the dripping fields, and played football in the mud most of the time while growing up. There were few of our contemporaries that didn't detest the seemingly constant downpour from October to May each year, and who wouldn't trade locales for anywhere that the sun shone most of the time.

I carefully steered the big '39 Lincoln Zephyr down Terwilliger Boulevard into the city. The streets were slick and the gutters were full with runoff from the showers. Our tires, like those on almost everyone's car, were already worn smooth due to the wartime shortage of new ones. It wouldn't do to have an accident while en route to apply for acceptance as pilot candidates in the U.S. Army Air Corps. It wouldn't look too good if you couldn't handle a car, and expect to be allowed to fly an airplane.

"There's the target at 3:00 o'clock," said Dave, who was "flying co-pilot" in the right seat. "It's that building there on the corner with the parking lot towards Burnside."

"Roger," I replied as 'First Pilot'. "We're 30 minutes ahead of our E.T.A., due no doubt to my superior flying and navigational ability."

"Yeh, sure," responded Dave. "You'd better hope your math and science subjects are more proficient if you expect to pass the qualification test for pilot training. I hear it's pretty tough."

Wheeling the bulky sedan into a parking stall, I turned to my companion. "You know, I'm not as worried about the written tests now as I am about the actual flying later. I'm not positive I'm even going to like it. I sure wish I'd had a chance before this to at least have had a ride in an airplane."

This would be the second Christmas during wartime that the Abners would observe. It didn't seem right somehow to do anything "as usual" when two members of our family and so many of our friends had sons or husbands in the service.

Not all of the Abner boys were subject to call for military service. My brother Paul, the one next to me, just nine years older, was truly the unlucky one of us. He'd developed arthritis at a very young age and was 4-F. It was the tragic event of his life. He was the best athlete of us all and was truly an All American young man. He watched his brothers go off to a war he was more than willing to fight. He could only remain at home, cheerfully silent yet supportive of our military careers.

Brother Burr, the eldest, enlisted in the air corps about the same time I did, though he was called up immediately. He chose not to try for a commission though he was a college graduate, but instead went for a technical career as a bombsight specialist.

Donald Adair, the second son, for some reason foreign to the rest of us landlubbers, chose the navy. His three years of college at the University of Oregon qualified him for officers' candidate school, and he was now an ensign in training at San Diego in PT Boats preparing for duty in the Pacific Theatre.

Our family was proud of the older sons' participation in the war effort, at the same time fearful of coming combat assignments. I was envious of them both and anxious to join them.

So far, I had not refused to honor my parents' wish that I go on to college after graduating from high school, and in the middle of my first year at Pacific College there were moments when I was glad to be where I was. I'd made varsity as a frosh on the football team, and was dreaming about becoming the Quakers' starting quarterback the next year if I returned.

That was the question. If I returned. Well, that question was answered now. I'd received my acceptance from the U.S. Army Air Corps that morning as a candidate for air cadet training as a pilot, and in two weeks would report for active duty at Sheppard Field, Texas.

Tonight I would tell Anna Laura of my decision, and that I'd soon be leaving.

Lolly, as I and her close friends call her, is almost two years younger than me, and though I'd known her since grade school, she'd always been more like a kid sister. As close neighbors we'd attended dozens of rodeos, games, dances, picnics and a variety of social events with our folks. It hadn't been until a year and a half ago when she graduated from Newberg High that I made a startling discovery.

It happened the night of her graduation ball. Or rather, it started when I stood in the vestibule of the Barnes's big old Victorian home waiting, corsage in hand, for my date for the event. I'd come to "pick up the kid" as I sometimes referred to her. But coming down the stairs was no "kid" in Levis and boots. This was a grown-up young lady who was an absolute knockout, dressed up like "Astor's Horse," as my grandad would have put it.

"No," I said to Lolly some weeks later when we were parked in the old cemetery up on the hill overlooking the town. "It was your hairdo more than anything else that really got to me. You know. You'd always wore it in that pony tail I used to tease you about. With your hair piled on top like you had it that night, you were suddenly someone new. Wow! Talk about a transformation. You weren't a kid anymore. And you sure as heck wasn't my kid sister."

"I'd stopped thinking of you as a Big Brother for quite some time before that night," said Lolly, smiling up at me. "You were just a little slow catching on. I figured it was time I gave you a little spur."

Once started, our romance flourished, and that summer and into the school year we were inseparable. Family occasions that up 'til then had been rather routine, suddenly took on different dimensions and provided new opportunities to be together. And of course, there were Sunday afternoons at the movies. And, Thursday's Dime Night at the Rex Theatre was rarely neglected. The routine was pretty much the same; the show itself with popcorn and Coke from the dispenser in the lobby. Then, hamburgers and shakes afterward at Bob's next door on Main Street. We'd been doing this ritual for years. But now it was different. Now we were pretty sure we were in love, and nothing was the same.

"I'm not sure when they'll let me come home on furlough," I told her as we sat huddled together in the big Lincoln sedan. A cold Oregon winter rain beat relentlessly on the windshield, and seemed somehow appropriate to this solemn pronouncement. "Dave got his notice the same day I did, so we'll be taking off at the same time. He's going to Arizona though, and I'm ordered to Wichita Falls, Texas. We'd kinda hoped we'd go to the same place. But no luck this time."

Lolly hadn't said anything when I'd told her about my call-up. It probably wasn't that there weren't a thousand things she'd thought of in the preceding months when she knew that this time would someday come. She said she'd thought she was prepared for this moment. But now that it was here, she just squeezed my hand and looked forlornly out the rain-streaked window.

"I don't want you to worry, Darlin'," I said as thousands of others like me were saying to their wives and sweethearts all over the world. "I'm going to be O.K. and you can bet your boots on it. And I'll write to you as often as I can. Why, I'll be home before you know it."

"I know," she said softly. "I'll be here when you get back."

CHAPTER II *TRAINING COMMAND–AIR CORPS*

There are no folks on earth more hospitable than Texans. Or "Texicans," as old cowboys used to call them. It wasn't the friendliness of the natives that was irksome. It was the confounded weather.

As an aviation cadet candidate I wanted to be a pilot, and pilots are by the nature of their trade very interested in weather. Flying weather, that is. And in February of that year of 1943, I was glad when my enlistment in the U.S. Army Air Corps had been accepted, and I'd been assigned to Wichita Falls, Texas for Basic Training. "Texas was south of Oregon, and it would be sunny, warm and dry. Right?"

Wrong. In the panhandle of Texas, where Sheppard Field was located, it was said you could stand up to your butt in mud, and a 50-mile per hour Norther would blow sand in your face. It was true. I and 1,200 other would-be aviation cadets, had the complexion to prove it.

Private Abner was assigned guard duty, and I was trying my best "to walk my post in a military manner," as the manual directed. Physically, I wasn't too uncomfortable. I had on more new clothes than I'd ever had in my life. The high top shoes were finally broken in after hours of daily drills and marches. The olive drab slicker reached almost to my knees, and the hard, dome-like helmet liner easily repelled the rain pellets that rattled like hail on a barn's tin roof. Even the carbine slung over my shoulder was not unlike the 410 shotgun that I'd carefully greased and stored in the gun case at the ranch. No, it wasn't too bad. Just kind of spooky.

15

North American Aviation–AT-6

Old cowpokes called them "Gully Washers." "Northers," was another southwestern name for the major storms that roared out of Canada and swept a path of destruction on their way to the Gulf of Mexico. The old days of trail herds and stampedes that exploded on stormy nights like this were long in the past. But it didn't take a lot of imagination to feel what it must have been like riding herd on a bunch of longhorns crazed with fear. My grandad had told me of the times in the early 1900s about riding herd on cattle drives from Texas to the rail heads in the North. The highlight of most of these yarns had centered on storms, cattle and stampedes. Tonite, these tales came to mind as I pounded my "beat" through the flooding streets of this huge, blackened army base.

From where I stood I could hardly make out the big water tank that rose on stilts some hundred feet above the acres of barracks that housed the enlistees quartered at Sheppard Field, Texas. The almost gale-force wind caused the rain not to fall, but rather to drive with furious intensity as tiny projectiles on a horizontal course. The low cloud, dimly lit by an occasional street light, scudded over the slumbering camp.

The highlight of the night came when "the vigilant sentry" challenged a command car that slowly made its way through the storm, headed for the center of the base where the command headquarters was located.

"Halt, who goes there? Advance and be recognized." It was the first "command" I'd ever uttered.

As the vehicle slowed to a stop, the rear window rolled down, and a shoulder displaying a silver eagle became visible in the dim light.

"Ah. What's the password? Sir?" My voice quavered a little.

"Yellow Rose," the "eagle" responded.

"Thank you, sir," I said. "Please proceed."

I stepped back, and throwing a salute at the now ascending window, watched with relief as the departing sedan splashed off into the storm.

"Migod! Wouldn't you know it! My first time out of the chute, and I draw the base commander," I muttered, recalling rodeo days. "That was a long ten seconds."

This night was the first time in seven weeks that I'd been alone. Days were crammed from before daylight until taps at night with a flurry of activity. There was no time to be homesick. There had been no time to just think since I left home.

When I left for active duty my mom and dad had driven me to the train station in Portland. My dad told me later that it wasn't until after I'd finally boarded, and the Portland Rose streamliner had pulled out, that my mother cried. Typically, the prayer she quietly said was not only that I return safely and unharmed, but that I brought honor to myself, to my family, and my country.

Earlier that day of departure, my dad and grandad had busied themselves with the precise loading of one suitcase and a toilet kit. Grandad took five minutes to load his crook-stem briar pipe, and his son rolled three cigarettes before he got it right. There just wasn't anything to say.

"God go with ye, me bye," the old man, who hadn't been to church in 40 years, said at last.

"We'll be here when you get back," said my dad, as he crushed my hand in his strong, brown paw.

The United States Army, like any military system since the beginning of history, knew how to convert young recruits from farm hands to fighting men. One secret was to keep them so busy that they had little time or enough remaining energy to dwell upon the relatively soft existence they'd left behind. Their entire consciousness was focused on NOW. Every drill, exercise, and command was designed to create a sort of automaton who would conform to the system, and would ultimately perform unthinkingly to the demands of combat. The system was working as planned with me, as it was with my fellow comrades in arms. Up until now I had been totally engrossed in the new demands and challenges that I was confronted with.

Tonight's guard duty assignment had appeared as just another new facet of being a soldier. But it was different. For one thing it was very quiet except for the storm. And I was alone. There had been many pre-dawn times when I'd trudged with Dad through the mud and rain to the barn for the start of another typical winter day on the ranch. This night in Texas, in a strange way, was suddenly familiar.

"In about two hours, it'll be time to start milkin'," I thought. "I wonder if Old Yeller has calved yet."

Great Britain's "good old boys" are fond of saying something about "The strength of the British Empire is built on the playing fields of Eton," or some such expression. Well, the Americans who planned the curriculum for the U.S. Aviation Cadet program, apparently were preparing the development of the strength of the whole world!

The hills of Texas rang from pre-dawn 'til dark with the strident cries and commands of drill sergeants, physical training officers, tactical officers, parade commanders and others getting those "gadgets" in shape. This was "Eton, USA," Pre-Flight, San Antonio, Texas.

And IN SHAPE we became. My 5 foot 11 inch frame had carried 168 pounds when I played on the Pacific College eleven. I then thought I was at my fighting weight. Now, at $160^{1}/2$ pounds, I knew I was. Two hours daily of close order drill on the parade ground, a weekly eight-mile cross-country run, and a two-hour parade on Saturdays, and you developed great leg muscles and almost flat feet. Two hours daily of calisthenics, with the weather hot or cold, wet or dry, and you developed whatever muscles you'd missed marching and drilling.

But it was not all tedious drudgery. Another hour devoted to one's physique was found in the 14-hour day to play. That's right, Play...and six-man cadet ball, or "touch football" was the favorite sport on the playing fields of Texas.

The "washing out" process we'd first experienced some weeks earlier in Basic Training continued now during Pre-Flight. And, the various ways you could get "washed out" were numerous. Unlike "Basic," all training here was not just physical. There was Ground School each weekday, and competitive scholastic ratings soon took on ominous proportions.

The various ways that air corps privates could be grounded forever, their dreams of being a pilot dashed, were wide ranging...returning minutes late from a rare eight-hour pass; lack of respect to a superior (drill sergeants, often with grade school educations); fighting with another airman; failure to maintain a competitive scholastic grade level; failure to pass frequent physicals, such as cross country runs against time, push-ups, rope climbs, obstacle course runs, and other endurance and skill competitions.

In one case, an apple left over from the evening's mess was hastily thrown into the owner's duffle bag while getting ready for the daily morning inspection of quarters. Its discovery qualified the airman to do four hours "on the ramp," after hours, marching up and down, with a seat-pack parachute strapped on his back and butt. Of course, this was corporal punishment! But it was the "privates" that got it.

Alan Abner at the Primary Flying School in 1943.

Thirty-five percent of the total class enrollment in Pre-Flight made it, me included. At last, flying school for us. The investment in effort had been so great until now, that no one was going to screw up if he could help it down the line.

"Off We Go."

Pre-Flight training at "San Antone" was over. Casey and I, and some 60 of our fellow privates who had survived the first screenings and wash-outs were assigned to the Primary Flying School at Ballinger, Texas, in the Air Training Command Southwest, whose flying schools were scattered throughout the state. We army privates were now air corps cadets, with new officer-type uniforms, and a raise in pay from $21.00 a month to $75.00, and at last we were going to leap into the "Wild Blue Yonder."

At Ballinger it was easy to imagine you were in a twilight zone of World War I. First, the open-cockpit airplanes. Then the flying garb! Heavy leather fleece-lined coats, pants and boots...leather helmets with goggles...and, of course, a flowing, white silk scarf.

Talk about fun! Two hours of dual instruction flying time each day, five days a week in the Fairchild PT-19. This exhilarating daily flying session consisted of learning all of the basic fundamentals of "Flying by the seat of your pants," take-offs and landings...aerobatics, that included snap rolls, barrel rolls, slow rolls, Immelmanns, chandelles, loops, spins and lazy eights. And, when you least expected it, a chopped throttle by the instructor...power off, and a simulated forced landing. You soon learned that no matter how hard you were concentrating on executing the maneuver of the moment, you must also have in mind an emergency landing field within your gliding range that you could reach, and safely make a dead-stick landing. Of course, before actually touching down, power would be restored and back to work aloft. "Forced Landings" was probably the one item on the instructor's daily grading record that was given the most weight. And it was possibly the one lesson that could serve an airman best at some time during his flying career.

Each phase of the cadet program, Primary, Basic and Advance, was burdened by the constant threat of getting "washed out." It could happen during the two hours the Primary cadets spent daily in the air. Four hours of Ground School required academic performance that became more and more competitive as the cadet progressed from one phase to another. Military bearing and behavior were now equally high on the list. Athletic ability, and the qualities of team play participation and leadership, in some cases determined a cadet's future assignment. There was little room for error.

"Mister Van Kleve was a no good, sadistic, sonofabitch!" I spoke quietly, but with feeling. "Anyone unlucky enough to get him for a Primary instructor is doomed for disaster!" I was one cadet that had no history of bad luck. In fact, I'd been pretty fortunate all of my life, 'til now! Why, I'd never even had a contagious disease while growing up. You could even say I'd been damn lucky to get Mr. Johnson for my first flight instructor. It was Mr. Johnson who had soloed me after only five hours of dual instruction in the Fairchild trainer. Mr. Johnson was an old barnstormer with, who knows, how many flying hours in his personal pilot's log book. He was a fatherly guy who patiently explained everything in great detail on the ground, and quietly and firmly demanded precise execution in the air. Mr. Johnson was a helluva good pilot, an excellent instructor, and a gentleman in the literal sense of the word. "Mr. Van Kleve was a no-good sonofabitch!"

Any cadet who got Mr. Van Kleve for an instructor soon echoed my sentiments with feeling. It turned out I was just being consistent.

"Have you ever really looked at that little twirp?" I asked of the small group of my fellows who were gathered in the P.X. after the evening chow to sip a soft drink, and review the adventures of the day. "My grandmother had a name for guys like him that fits him like a glove...a popinjay! That's what he is, a blasted popinjay! Mr. Van Kleve is Mr. 'Vain' Kleve, that's what he is!"

My biased description was not too inaccurate. The instructor under discussion was a civilian as were the other Primary School instructors, but all of them were bestowed with the status of military officer personnel, and enjoyed the courtesies extended to the officers. They were issued uniforms similar to those worn by airline captains of the time. Some of them wore these duty outfits with a casual air, as if they, as old flying hands, didn't much care about military spit and polish. Others effected an almost "West Point air," and were inclined to strut rather than stroll. Van Kleve surpassed this latter group.

This instructor was a slight, tough, wiry little man, five feet four or five inches in height, and weighed probably no more than 150 pounds. A swarthy complexion was capped by coal black, rather longish hair (long for a West Point grad), and beneath his hawk nose was a carefully trimmed mustache, like those favored by movie idols of the time, like Ramon Navarro and Warner Baxter. He didn't carry a swagger stick, but you knew he would have liked to.

"He is exactly what he looks like," I continued..."He can fly a little, but he sure as hell can't teach it. All he does is prance around the base and chew on you in the air in that nasty bitchy way of his. It's bad enough on the ground where he's careful that the other instructors might hear him. But, in the air, he really pulls out all of the stops...'you're the most stupid cadet I've ever had'...'you'll never be a pilot'...'you couldn't drive a nail'...'I could teach an ape to fly easier than I could ever teach a numbskull like you!'... ad nauseum."

After enduring my instructor's thinly disguised hazing for more than a month, this day promised to be the worst yet. As usual, I got off on the wrong foot. This time, by having given, as "Mr. Vain" said, a sloppy salute when he reported to the flight line. Although I had been getting passing average grades on his flight tests, it was getting tougher and tougher to cope with the personal harassment I was subjected to. "Boy, today's going to be a real dandy," I said to myself.

This prediction for that date proved to be an understatement. Instructor Van Kleve reached new heights in verbal abuse...Nothing was right. Everything his student pilot did, met with increasingly vitriolic invective. Finally, he said the magic words.

"You goddamn stupid sonofabitch!"

As these words sizzled through the intercom, I, as they say, came unglued. On the ranches and small towns of Oregon from which I sprang, these were fighting words. I'd put up with a lot of sarcastic abuse with reference to my brains, my talent, or my skills. But my lineage was not a topic to be tolerated. This Welsh-Irishman boiled over.

The blind rage that enveloped me did not slow my reaction. Carefully I reached up and disengaged the connecting intercom speaking tubes from my helmet, shutting off the voice that was still screaming from the rear cockpit. Reaching down, I clasped the stick control with two strong, young hands. With adrenalin flowing like hot lava, I began to rapidly bang the control column from side to side, causing the aircraft to rock and roll like a storm-tossed dingy in the sea.

It was what was happening in the rear cockpit that most interested me. "Mr. Vain," seated in the narrow cramped quarters, could not stop, could not even grasp the increasingly rapid, back and forth motion of the stick that was beating the hell out of his defenseless knees. Back and forth! again, again, and again!

Finally, cooling a little, I released my hold on my half of the dual control sticks. The training plane slowly regained the more reasonable attitude any casual outside observer would expect from a pilot and instructor flight. Mr. Van Kleve, again in control of the craft, carefully guided the descending trainer aircraft back to the home field. Nothing was said between student and instructor. The intercom was still disconnected!

Resigned, but not contrite, I knew I would be washed out. "C'est la guerre."

Although I had written to Lolly every week since I'd been gone, this letter was going to be tough to write. Up 'til now my accounts had been full of self-confidence and enthusiasm as I progressed from being a boot-private, to my present status as a real aviator. She'd said in her response that my letter written to her on the day I'd soloed had "thrilled her with the exuberance it transmitted to her world."

This letter was going to be tough to write.

Saturday

Dearest Lolly,

Well, it hasn't happened yet but it looks like you and Mom won't have to worry about my flying any more. Don't tell her now, but I expect I'll be washed out of the cadet program come Monday. I wish I could tell you it was someone else's fault, but it really isn't. I guess my Irish temper just caught up with me at the wrong time. Grandad always warned me to look out for it. He never said so, but I suspect his temper was the cause of his losing that chunk out of his right ear. Well, I wish it was only my ear lobe I'd lost. And just when I was really getting the hang of this flying business.

I won't get into a lot of details now as I expect I may be seeing you sooner than we expected. Just let me say that I got an instructor that was a lot like that greasy haired transient your Dad had to whip and run off the ranch that year you were about twelve. My guy wasn't as big as the one your Dad dealt with, but if anything he was twice as mean. I put up with a lot more abuse from him than I ever thought I would from any man, but he finally got to me when he got a little personal.

I'm not too sorry I did what I did. I wouldn't be surprised if I would do it over again if anything like it would happen to me again.

But that doesn't change things. The Army's dead set against any kind of conflict between the troops, and especially between a "Gadget" and a superior. There are cadets getting washed out every day for a lot less, so I don't expect I'll be an exception.

You're the only one I've told about this. I haven't said a word even to my bunk mates. So, come Monday, when they give me my walkin' papers, I'll ride off into the sunset like the Duke.

Don't worry Darlin'. I've been throwed before, but I've always managed to get another mount. Can't wait to see you. You're always on my mind. Love and kisses.

Case

Air Training Command regulations, indeed, all military regulations forbid the use of verbal, profane abuse of any man by a superior regardless of rank. This fact may have occurred to Mr. "Vain" Kleve while he was applying hot packs and poultices to his black and blue knees and legs. This "unlucky" cadet was immediately assigned to another instructor. This time my luck held, and my grades and proficiency soared. This incident did not even appear in my Personal History 201 Military File. There is military justice it seems.

Phase Two, Basic Training was the same Ground School and physical and flying curriculum for the advancing cadets who had survived Primary. But, one thing was greatly improved. It was considerably warmer. Gone was the romantic World War I "pursuit plane" with its open cockpit. Instead, here now was a modern low-wing monoplane with a plexiglass "bird cage" canopy...Gone was the World War I intercom Gosport tube that allowed the instructor to talk to his student in the front seat. This had been accomplished by the simple device of a rubber hose extending from the funnel held to the lips of the instructor in the rear seat, extending to the split ends of the tube that were attached to the helmet and ears of the student in front. The Basic instructor was just as tough and demanding as his predecessor, but now he chewed you out on a radio.

The plane looked huge after the kites we'd been flying. Instead of fabric, the fuselage, wings, everything was shining aluminum. And the engine was a monster by comparison. The BT-13 trainer was called the "Vultee Vibrator."

My first indoctrination flight with my instructor, Mr. Duby, was to be a day I would long remember. Although I had become academically familiar with the BT-13 in Ground School, actually getting into the bird, and flying it was all I had anticipated. Mr. Duby had demonstrated and then allowed me to execute power-on and power-off stalls, spins to the right and left, and then had given an aerobatics exhibition that showed this young birdman what this aircraft could and couldn't do. I was impressed.

After an aerial tour of the surrounding terrain, pointing out landmarks that would later be useful on solo flights and cross country's, we returned to Brady Field, and obtained clearance to join the landing pattern, where others were flying the rectangular course. Entering on a 45-degree angle to the downwind leg, Mr. Duby spaced our craft some quarter of a mile from the trainer preceding us. As we turned left onto our base leg, we both noticed two planes on the final approach ahead of us!

The lower BT was "dragging it in," under power, about one hundred feet off the ground. Slightly behind and above, a second trainer was in a typical, steep, power-off, nose slightly raised glide towards the end of the runway.

Neither I nor my instructor said a word during the few seconds we watched in horror as the top craft landed squarely atop the lower plane just as its wheels touched on the runway.... It was no surprise when we later learned that the student and the instructor in the first plane were both killed.

Flying was great fun. Flying was also a deadly, unforgiving taskmaster.

The entire air corps cadet training routine in flying schools, as it was from the very beginning back in Pre-Flight, left very little time for introspection. Day-dreaming, mooning around or crying in one's beer was not done, at least openly. Each day's schedule required dedicated concentration whether it was in the classroom, the cockpit or on the playing field. Except for the lucky few who happened to have kin living within a few hours' distance from the base where they were stationed, the vast majority had not been home for over a year. It was natural that these 18- and 19-year-old cadets, most of whom had never been away from home at all until now, would have gotten homesick. Some did. But it didn't last long. They just didn't have time for it.

Saturdays were "down time," no flight instructions, but full-dress parades, and athletic contests were the order of the day. A Saturday night pass for those who hadn't "goofed" during the week was issued.

Sundays were free-time after reveille, morning chow and inspection of quarters. Much of the day was devoted to studying Ground School assignments. But for a few precious moments, there came a late afternoon or evening bull session.

Like my grandad, I liked to tell a story. I wasn't big for tales of my romantic prowess, a popular topic. But I did love to reminisce about "when I was a kid." This, of course, was four or five years ago.

This Sunday was a rare day in Brady, Texas. It was raining. Not an endless northwest rainy day that poured and drizzled forever. No, this was a line squall series of thunderheads that dumped gallons of water at almost scheduled intervals. It was a day, however, that reminded me of an earlier adventure, "when I was a kid."

The half-inch galvanized pipe was about six inches long. Doubling a rawhide bootlace, I knotted it about six inches from the loop end and threaded the two loose ends through the pipe, leaving a 10-inch loop of leather. I then tied the two loose ends with a knot almost as big as the pipe, and cut off the rawhide that was left over. The pipe was then inserted into a piece of garden hose just the right diameter to provide a tight rubber cover over the pipe. And there it was. A homemade "sap," in case I ever needed one.

I had made that "silent persuader" just a couple of weeks before, getting ready to head out to see the world, or more accurately, the San Francisco World's Fair that was going on some six hundred miles south of our ranch in Newberg, Oregon. I'd never been very far away from home other than occasional trips to Portland, which was 26 miles away. My "thumb" had got me there a few times, and I figured it would get me to the Golden Gate.

I'd told my folks I was going to Corvallis to visit with a neighbor boy who was finishing his spring term at Corvallis where Oregon State Agriculture College was located. O.S.C. was only 80 some miles away, so nobody objected too much. My brother was home for the summer, so Dad would have help with the chores I usually did.

I did spend the first night with my friend, but the next morning I headed walking out of town in order to get on Highway 99, the main inland route to California, where the cars would be heading that way, and not just going to work.

I looked pretty good as hitchhikers go. I'd brought along an old college "beanie" that my older brother had acquired when he was a college freshman. My windbreaker was green, a local college color, and my corduroy pants were clean. My only luggage was a small zipper bag that held a change of shorts, sox, a sweater, a pair of light khaki pants, swimming trunks, and a pair of sneakers. My "sap" was handy in my jacket pocket. Oh yes, I almost forgot about my Frank Medico briar pipe, and the can of Half and Half tobacco. I hadn't learned to inhale yet, but as an aspiring actor, I felt the pipe lent a certain mature, romantic air. When you're 16 years old, props are getting important. There was also a Gillette razor and a pack of Blue Blades that I assembled and used once or twice a week, whether I needed a shave or not.

Rides were scarce in spite of my role as a college boy on his way home for the summer vacation. There were a lot of real college boys with their thumbs out, and most of the cars were full. It was late afternoon and I'd only travelled one hundred miles or so to the town of Drain. The town was well named as it had started to rain; a cold, blustery, unseasonable rain for anyplace but Oregon, and it was getting late in the day.

It was here I decided to leave Highway 99, and cut over to the Pacific Coast, through the Coast Range to Reedsport some 70 miles away. The weather might be better, and though the Coast Highway was not as busy as the main inland route, I might get away from the competition.

It started out as I hoped. I hadn't even stuck out my thumb, when an old pickup truck stopped, and I climbed in with an old guy who was obviously a rancher of some kind. We didn't talk much as we travelled through the now pouring rain, as the pickup made quite a racket, and the driver was pretty deaf.

I hadn't asked him how far he was going, so it was something of a surprise when he turned into a dirt road that led up a mountain, stopped, and let me off. I figured we had come about 40 miles. I was about halfway to Reedsport, it was now pretty dark, and it was really pouring. There was no traffic.

Well, nothing to do but hoof it. I'd gone only a short distance when I could see a shed set back maybe 20 or 30 feet from the road. I don't to this day know what it had been used for, but I strongly suspect it had been a holding place for pigs ready to be picked up and shipped to market. I was familiar with pig smell. We'd raised our own meat at home. Luckily, this sty hadn't been used for some time. It was dry and fairly tight, but a memory lingered on, left by its previous inhabitants. The aroma didn't bother me so much that I didn't doze off during the long night, but at first light I was out on the road again headed west. At least it had stopped raining.

A milk truck picked me up before I'd gone a mile. The driver was really a nice guy, and when he learned we had a dairy and a creamery in Newberg, he went all out. He gave me a couple of extra donuts he carried for his breakfast, which I washed down with a quart of milk that tasted even better than ours. A half pint of Bireley's orange juice, and I was ready for anything.

Heading south an hour or so later, the walk out of Reedsport was a breeze, and it was no time 'til I got another lift.

Another pickup truck. I tossed my bag in the truck bed's right front corner as I got aboard. The driver was a young guy, probably in his middle twenties, and was what my dad would call "a rough looking hombre." He wore a dirty undershirt, though it was not warm enough to not wear a shirt, even a jacket. He had dark, kind of dank long hair, and he smoked one cigarette after another, taking the one out of his mouth, and lighting each new one off the short butt of the old one.

I was kind of nervous. He was a new breed that I'd never run into. He asked a lot of questions; 'How old was I,' all mixed up with some cuss words I hadn't heard before.

We passed through and had just reached the edge of the little town of Lakeside when he pulled over on a graveled lookout point overlooking a little bay that offered a good look at the Pacific Ocean. He turned to me and laid a hand on my left wrist, and put a really good grip on it.

"O.K. kid. You've got to have some money, and I mean to be paid for the ride. Hand it over!"

Strangely enough, I wasn't really scared. He was trying to look real mean, but his jaw was quivering, and his eyes looked kinda scared.

What happened then worked so good, later I could hardly believe it.

I had my hand in the right pocket of my jacket, and the loop of my 'sap' was around my wrist. I pulled it out suddenly, and with all my might, I cracked him right on the back of his hand that was clamped onto my wrist.

He let out a yell, and as he let go, I got out of that cab, grabbed my bag out of the truck bed, and took off back toward Lakeside, running like a deer. There was a service station only a block or so away and I pulled up there and looked back. The pickup was pulling out back on the highway still headed south, lurching and jumping like the driver might be having a little trouble working the gear shift with a busted right hand.

"I may be a sap for doing this, but that 'sap' I've got in my pocket sure did the trick," I said to myself. It was the only time I ever used it. It's still in a box in the attic with some other stuff I brought home from the World's Fair. But without it, the other things wouldn't be there.

At last came the final stages of cadet training. I, and some two hundred other survivors of the ten months of concentrated flying, physical and mental exertions, were now just 28 days from graduation. Victoria, Texas was the site of Aloe Field, the Advance Training Base where we would get our wings if we were successful. Of course, final grades and ratings were the most important items on everyone's list. But not far behind in things to be accomplished, was the winning of the Group's Cadet Football Championship. Flight A, 81st Squadron, my team, was in the home stretch scheduled for the semi finals.

Aloe Field was situated on the outskirts of an unusually beautiful east Texas town. Victoria, Texas was more deep-south than the cow-towns scattered throughout the state. Ante bellum homes, gracious vine-covered Victorians, and quiet, shady streets reminded one of Atlanta or Tallahassee. And, Aloe Field was also unique. The air base had an athletic field that had GRASS.

Six-man cadet football was a wide open, running and passing game. Playing positions included a center; a quarterback, whose position was played in the shotgun stance; two blocking backs, and two wide end receivers. Every player could catch a pass, every player could throw a pass from anyplace on the field, and the team, on any down, could throw as many times as they could get away with it before they were tagged.

I'd been chosen as the quarterback of my flight's team, and I'd done pretty good. I didn't have the running speed of a sprinter, but I was fairly quick and agile. And, as a passer, I could drill a rifle shot at close range, or unload a bomb in the 40-yard vicinity.

The other semi-finalist team in the 83rd Squadron was our rival, C Flight, led by quarterback Joe Hibbs, who was himself a ring-tailed wonder. But the star of this sextet was a tall, lanky, whipcord-tough, six-foot drink-of-water named John Casey.

This cadet was cadet major commanding his squadron; he was an outstanding student, and to cap it all off, he was an all-round athlete. He excelled in any sport, but more important to the moment, he'd been an All American Mention his sophomore year at the University of Ohio where he'd played end. In college, Casey had brought a refinement to his position that was unique in those days of the single wing. He was not only a very fast receiver, but he had sticky hands that caught enough passes to shatter all of the Buckeyes' aerial reception records. This talent alone was enough to get national attention. But he had another skill that would have made him a number one draft pick by any of the professional football coaches. He was absolutely devastating as a pass rusher on defense. Quick as a cutting horse, he dodged and crashed his way to ensnare more quarterbacks with his long, rawhide tough arms than anyone in the Big 10 could remember. John Casey was the franchise. And that day, A Flight knew it.

The hot Texas sun was slanting toward the purpling hills to the west. It had been a long, hot, frustrating afternoon for A Flight... The crowd, cadets, enlisted personnel, officers and townies were beginning to think about drifting away to the shade and finding a cold one. We still gamely toiled on in what was now a losing battle. Twenty-eight to 13 was no shellacking, but it was not a win either. And I did not like to lose at anything.

Came the snap, and I faded back, drifted a little to my right waiting for my receiver to get deep down field. Again, here came Casey. Clemson, our weary left-half blocking back was still no match for the charging defensive end. Almost instantly, Casey was scant feet from me as I was being blind-sided while releasing my throw. As the ball left my hand, Casey, forgetting for an instant this wasn't the Big Ten, flung out his long right arm to block the pass. Instead, his elbow curled around my neck as he crashed into the back of my slightly bent figure. I didn't go down, though my knees buckled under the weight of this unseen assailant. It wasn't a "dirty shot"...nor was it touch football. I'm afraid I reacted immediately and violently.

The day's frustrations already had my reflexes tuned to a high pitch. Before my face was the long bony wrist of the enemy. Grabbing it with both hands, I pulled down with all of my bunched up strength, and executed a perfect, though ad-lib, judo fall. Casey, thus propelled, did an inside loop over my head, straightened out in mid air, and came crashing to the soft turf, flat on his back. Stunned from the swift force of the retaliation, his wind knocked out, Casey looked up, and he saw the blood-blackened face of a furious cadet ...legs apart, fists clenched, awaiting for his foe to get to his feet.

Cadet Casey...Quarterback Abner...heard the whistle.

"I suggest you both hit the showers, and get cooled off." The P.T. Officer did not make this statement as a request. It was a direct order, and neither of us misread his intent. The athletic officer did not appear to be angry. His manner indicated no emotion at all. He was "correct," as they say. And we headed out towards the field house, heads down, like a couple of truant schoolboys.

We both remained silent as we toweled dry after our "cooling off" therapy. We each held the same chilling thought as we slowly dressed. Washed Out. Two words; like Too Old, Too Dumb or Too Late. Two words that could pronounce a sentence too devastating to contemplate. And we both had done the unthinkable...we had lost control.

Our fears were well founded. We'd both known cadets who had been eliminated for far less serious offenses. We knew the odds. One out of five of all those entered in the Aviation Cadet program ultimately won their wings. And an equally small number of those survivors made fighter pilot.

"Boy, we really blew it," Casey exclaimed, finally breaking the ice. "Imagine, after all we've been through, to screw up over a lousy football game."

I regarded my now partner-in-crime with sardonic amusement. "At least, you won the game," I stated flatly.

"To hell with the game," growled Casey. "Win the game, and lose the cause. Get benched for good, and end up flying a goddamn desk!"

The two of us, now dressed smartly in crisp summer cottons, grommeted hats set squarely on our heads academy style, shoes gleaming, marched at parade pace across the quadrangle to the barracks.

"Well, old buddy," I said, sticking out my hand, "we'll know soon enough I guess. Graduation is less than a month now. They surely won't let us sweat it out that long."

Casey put a little extra squeeze in his grip. "Well, at least we got to know each other. You're a helluva quarterback, you know it. And I'll bet you're not too bad in the air either. Maybe we'll meet in the Wild Blue Yonder yet."

We both grinned a little at this hackneyed public relations reference.

"Yeah, 'Off We Go'," I quoted. "Where, is the question. I just hope they don't drag it out. They couldn't let us sweat it out for a whole month, could they?"

But they did.

Victoria, Texas

Dear Lolly,

I guess I told you how great it was to get assigned here for advance training. It's been everything I'd hoped. I really feel sorry for the boys that were assigned to twin engine schools after Basic. I was sure lucky again. As you know, we're flying single engine planes and of course that means if we're good enough, and if nothing happens, we could get assigned to fighters when we graduate. That's a lot of ifs for sure, so cross your fingers.

I hope I don't bore you with all my talk about flying and airplanes, but except for thinking about you and home, I don't think much of anything else.

I just can't get over how much fun flying the AT-6 is. Boy, those North American Aircraft guys sure know how to build an airplane. They also make the P-51 Mustang fighter, and if it's anything like the T-6 it's got to be a wonder.

Almost all of our daily flying is done solo now except for instrument and instruction check rides. We've really been trained in almost every phase of combat flying and occasionally a night cross country. What's really fun is to arrange it with a close buddy and meet in the air off in a remote area and have a mock Dog Fight. The instructors know we do it even if it's not part of the official schedule. But you really practice almost all of the aerobatic tricks you've learned, and there's no greater feeling than getting on your "enemy's" trail and not get shook off. I can't wait to try it in a real fighter.

By the way, we do have four P-40s, Warhawks, real fighter planes stationed here at Aloe, and we're scheduled to get checked out in them before graduation. I've spent some time just sitting in one parked on the ground and learning the check list we'll have to know and do blindfolded before they turn us loose. It's kind of an ugly buzzard when it's not flying, but boy, it's a vicious looking machine when those instructors come in on the deck and make a tactical landing. Wow! I can hardly wait.

I just got back from evening mess. Food's pretty good. I still drink lots of milk. My barracks is empty. Most of the guys have gone into Victoria, tomorrow being Sunday. I'm kind of pooped. It's been a long day...parade, football game, etc., etc. Sure do miss you.

I don't know how to tell you this. But it seems like I've been doing this all of my life. It's so different from everything I did before. I wasn't sure I'd like the spit and polish of cadet life. I wasn't even sure I'd like to fly. But darned if I want to do anything else right now. Of course we think and talk about the war going on. But somehow it's not the terrible thing happening that it really is. I don't know of any of us who secretly or otherwise isn't just aching to get into it. I'm sure as hell (oops. I find myself swearing more lately. Don't tell Mom) not bloodthirsty or all that anxious to kill someone, but I sure believe in what we're fighting for, and those German and Jap bastards have to be stopped.

Sorry. I never talk like that to anyone. But with you, it somehow seems O.K. and that you'll understand.

Maybe it's because it's Saturday night, and we're not going to a dance or the movies, or most of all, not parked up on Cemetery Hill. We'll do that again someday, I promise.

All my love,
Alan

P.S. Sure appreciate the photographs you sent. The picture of Grandad with the milk pail on his head, and Dad holdin' him up at "gunpoint" with a broom aimed at him is really funny. Even Mom looks amused. Thanks.

Dear Don,

Sorry I haven't written more. It's not because I don't think about you and wonder how you're getting along. But you know how busy it can get after the time you spent in O.C.S. Besides, you owe me a letter.

I saw a guy yesterday in Victoria. He was an Ensign like you. Migod, you guys sure go around looking like Chaplains or even undertakers in those dark uniforms. I'll have to admit there's no doubt you're officers. An enlisted man wouldn't be caught dead in an outfit like that. I did salute this guy however. He looked kind of surprised. His girlfriend looked real pleased.

I'll bet you're having fun in those PT boats. It seems strange you being a sailor surrounded by all that water. No odder than me flying airplanes I guess. How did a couple of cowpokes like us make such strange career changes?

I'm due to graduate in a few weeks now. I almost hope I get my gold bars before you get promoted to J.G. I know that's selfish, but I would like to catch up with you just once. Though I guess it wouldn't hurt me to throw you a salute too.

Your combat assignment will be somewhere in the Pacific Theatre I suppose. I can't say I envy that. I have never liked the ocean or salt water since that summer at Cannon Beach when I got caught in the surf and that undertow. I've never been so scared. When you and that lifeguard threw that life preserver to me and dragged me in on the rope, I swore I'd never swim in anything deeper than an irrigation ditch again. And I haven't! I might have known the way you took to deep sea fishing that you'd thrive on it. You can have it!

I'm really hoping I get assigned to the European Theatre, assuming of course, that I get my wings. Not just because we'd be flying over land instead of water, but I've really developed a genuine distaste for the Nazis, to put it mildly. I surely despise the Japs for what they did to us at Pearl Harbor, and the way they fight this way. But I can't help but think of them as little yellow ignorant creeps who blindly obey their goddamn Emperor and have to be stamped out like fire ants. And that Kamikaze shit. Holy Cow!

But those Krauts are a different breed of cats. They sure as hell ain't stupid. They're smart, sadistic sons a bitches from the lowest private on up. We shouldn't be surprised how popular Hitler is with the Germans. Their whole history is full of aggressions against anyone weaker than they were. And Boy! You talk about exterminating their enemies. We've been getting some films (I don't think this is classified) on their concentration camps and it's enough to turn your stomach. Some behavior from a "Super Race!" One of our guys the other night during a bull-session said the Krauts were just like a bunch of sheep who blindly do what they're told. That's pure crap and I said so. I'm convinced there's something in the character of the German race that assures them from birth that they're superior to any other people and with that arrogance, they look for a leader like Shickelgruber who tells them they're right. They love it! And they're not happy unless they're goose-stepping on the necks of people who don't agree with them.

Good God. I didn't mean to get so wound up. But I'll tell you. Knowing who your enemy is and hating him enough to kill him sure gives you an incentive to learn how to do it.

Otherwise, what else is new? How's your love life? I suppose you're still using that "Oh, I'm just a single ole country boy crap." I won't argue that you seemed to have pretty good luck with it. It's just that it always made me want to throw up in the back seat.

Try to behave, Pard.

Best of luck,
Alan

CHAPTER III *FIGHTER AIRCRAFT–AT LAST*

Alphabetically my name, Alan K. Abner, preceded John L. Casey's on the list. Shoulder to shoulder, we two "combatants" pushed and shoved our way through the crowd of cadets in a manner unbecoming officers and gentlemen.

There it was. Both names, with rank and serial numbers listed. Pilots. Second lieutenants in the United States Army Air Corps.

And there, next to this roster was another list that designated the next assignment for duty.

We stood, stunned in disbelief. Ramrod straight, we stared in an almost hypnotic trance at the now blurring bulletin.

"Holy cow," I whispered. "Can you believe it? We got fighters! We got fighters," I repeated stupidly.

Casey turned his eyes to face me. "We got fighters," he repeated in awed disbelief. "Not only did we not get washed out, we got fighters!"

Years later, I would learn that our P.T. football incident had *supported* the promotion board's consideration to select us as fighter pilots. In addition to the vast criteria of elements accumulated during the various phases of the pilot training program, personality traits were high on the list. Fighter pilots were men who flew alone, without the moral support of a crew. They were navigators, gunners, bombardiers and pilots rolled into one individual. Their psychological make-up included behavioral characteristics that would support a combat performance that, if not pugnacious, was adequately aggressive, and almost always individually initiated and executed.

Curtis Warhawk P-40

Again, two usually undemonstrative men shook hands, this time each gripping with all of his might. For a long few seconds our eyes were locked together. Without a word, we broke apart, and easing through the still pressing crowd, went away, each to his own private place where this wonderful happening could be put into a rational perspective. After all, officers were expected to behave with dignity. And fighter pilots were cool.

The teeth in the mouth of that voracious deep sea predator were almost a foot long. The white jagged row of razor sharp incisors ran clear from the snout of that long torpedo-like head, back some six or seven feet almost to the leading edge of the wing. It was not a flying fish, though it did look more like a shark than a tiger. "Flying Tiger." That's the name that Chennault's guys flying in the China-Burma Theatre in the early stages of the war had called themselves. And the P-40 Warhawk was renamed. "Pappy" Boington and his "Misfits" had played hell with the Japanese Zeros, and tales of their exploits were the favorite topic in every fighter pilot Ready Room in the Training Command.

My new instructor for this transition into combat aircraft had actually flown with the "Tigers." He'd made captain, and the ribbons on the chest of his Class A uniform more than supported the fact he was a two-times Ace.

"I know you guys had 10 hours or so in the P-40 after you graduated back at Advance," Captain "Torry" Torrance said to the four young pilots who faced him. "You're going to fall in love with this baby, and it's going to scare hell out of you before you're done. You can't see a damn thing in front on final approach because of the nose; the bird cage canopy will sure develop your eyesight; and she drops like a rock, power off, or in a nose-down position. The landing gear is what you might call narrow, and if you're not good at power-on wheel landings, you soon will be."

Torry Torrance was right. I, like the others, took to this combat-tested "Tiger" like ducks take to water.

I gained an instant liking for the Curtis Warhawk P-40 fighter during that brief 10 hours of transition back to Aloe. My first flight, solo of course in that single seater, held for me the same thrills it did for the other cadets on their initial maiden flight in a fighter.

It was five miles after take-off before I tentatively lifted the gear. Then a cautious, gradual climb as I carefully put in the proper trim and power settings. And, another 10 miles before I tried a shallow turn to the left, and felt myself slightly greying-out with the unaccustomed G-Forces. "Wow! What a bird this baby is!"

After gaining sufficient altitude, I then went through the usual check-out maneuvers I'd become accustomed to earlier in the three phases of flying schools when checking out in the Fairchild, the BT-13, and the AT-6.

At the debriefing conducted by my instructor upon landing, I reported on my first flight. "Take-off wasn't too good," I began. "I only tried one needle-width turn. Power on and power off stalls were really pretty easy. Three turn spins to the left recovered easily, but the spins to the right were a little hairy, but I came out O.K. I lost quite a bit of altitude, but...."

"You what?" It was almost a scream. "You spun to the right and..." the instructor was actually sputtering. "You never spin a fighter," he yelled. "Goddamn it, I would have thought you knew that!"

I did not know that. It had never been mentioned in the pre-flight briefings. I knew it now! I also knew how the P-40 Warhawk behaved in a spin recovery. Later, I was glad I did.

The combat transition training period at Dale Mabry Field in Tallahassee, Florida continued throughout the hot, sultry summer. Torry Torrance patiently coached us in formation flying, cross countries, night maneuvers, air combat techniques and tactics, and what was perhaps the most fun of them all: aerial gunnery.

Shooting at ground targets at Matagorda Island down in the Gulf of Mexico during Advance Transition had been great. But to me and the others, the most exciting target practice was that to be found at 12 to 14,000 feet, firing on a target sleeve towed by an instructor-piloted aircraft.

The aerial gunnery pattern was really pretty routine. Four fighters set up in a rectangular pattern, flying at intervals, one at a time, down on a long leg of the pattern, until the target plane approached at a slightly lower altitude, heading in the opposite direction, coming towards them. The fighter then turned toward the oncoming target, timing his turn so that he closed at approximately a 30-degree angle to the target now going away. When in range, and having set up the deflection lead on the target, with the use of a circle on the windshield lined up on a beaded pin on the nose of the P-40, the target was fired upon with the 30-calibre machine guns in their wing mounts. Hits on the sleeve were recorded by dabs of each pilot's color left on the sleeve by the paint that coated their projectiles.

Altitude deflection gunnery was fun, and required a great deal of concentration, and some good flying technique.

I was better than average; this day I felt I was hot. I'd made three passes and on each one made strikes on the target. "Everything was swell! I was probably the best fighter pilot in the world! I was practically an ace!!" I actually giggled in the exuberance of the moment...as I passed out.

The world had gone crazy! I was in the middle of a tornado! As my vision cleared I found myself still in the P-40, but it was like no aircraft I'd ever been in. I was falling and spinning. The engine was roaring, the cockpit was filled with flying debris: maps, tubes and wire, dust, and a million little flying objects swirling about. My feet were off the rudders, my knees up around my waist. Even my arms were forced toward the roof of the tiny cabin, the backs of my wrists touching the clammy canopy.

I was plunging toward the earth in an inverted spin.

While completing the aerial gunnery exercise at 14,000 feet, I'd had a failure in the oxygen supply system. A lack of oxygen causes some strange and insidious sensations. The victim doesn't feel bad, he feels good. Very Good! Anoxia is very much like the early euphoric stages of an alcoholic binge, then advances quickly to unconsciousness. As I regained my senses and as my altitude rapidly decreased, the next few vital moments could best be described in milli-seconds.

"I'm in a spin. Migod, I'm in an inverted spin!" This was the maneuver no one ever practiced...especially in a high performance fighter plane. There had been conversations about recovery from this treacherous condition... "But, how did it go?"

Demanding my muscles to perform against the tremendous pressures exerted by the negative "G's" produced by the plane's action, I forced my feet onto the rudder pedals; at the same time bringing my right hand down to the stick, and the left hand to the throttle quadrant.

First...cut off power.

Now, grab the stick with both hands, and ONE...pull it as hard as possible back into my crotch...TWO, and THREE...jamb the rudder pedal in the direction of the spinning turn of the aircraft, and WAIT...A split second...It worked!

P-40 "Flying Tigers"

The aircraft snapped into a conventional spin, and this created a recovery maneuver I did know how to do. I'd "practiced" it my first time up in a P-40!

The P-40 Warhawk did "drop like a rock." This almost fatal accident had started out at 14,000 feet. When I pulled out of the now controllable dive, I was less than 100 feet from being "deep in the heart of Texas."

The debriefing of my mission, conducted by Captain Torrance, was well attended by all of the student pilots on base at Dale Mabry Field, and nearly all of the instructors.

"All I can say," Captain Torrance began, "is that you're shot in the ass with luck, Lieutenant Abner...I'm not saying that you didn't do a helluva job of flying. You did. When you finally 'sobered up,' you kept your cool, and, Lord knows, you did everything right. For the rest of you, you know there's a lot to learn from this inverted spin recovery. I wouldn't suggest you actually practice what you've learned, however. It isn't habit forming."

Tallahassee, Florida, in the summer is not a favorite retreat for northern vacationers. Oh, the temperatures are not too bad, but the humidity is pretty fierce. We new second lieutenants learning our trade as "pursuit pilots," as the old-timers still called us, were finally at the stage of our military careers where flying was principally what we did. We still had some ground school scheduled, and a parade on Saturday, but the P-40 Warhawk demanded most of our attention.

Off-duty hours were spent arguing the merits of the different fighter airplanes we might be assigned in combat. Our comments ran the gamut:

"I just hope I get a bird with an in-line engine like the P-40s we're flying. A Mustang. Now there's a real mean machine. At the right altitude they can whip anything the Krauts have got."

"Oh, sure. If we get sent to the 9th Air Force and ground support missions, you can get knocked down with a BB gun. Those liquid cooled engines are great for high altitude escort, but for strafing locomotives all it takes is one little coolant leak and you've bought it."

"Yeah. I'll take a T-Bolt and that huge air-cooled radial engine for that duty. You know, there's guys who've lost two or three cylinders and still make it back. Talk about a work horse."

"Boy, you guys talk like it's a cinch we're going to the E.T.O. and join the Limeys fighting the Luftwaffe. There's still a war going on in the Pacific, you know. And if we go there with all the missions over water, I'd kind a like another engine on my bird. Maybe a P-38 if there's any left."

I rarely joined in these sometimes heated arguments. I was as much in the dark as the next in having any advance knowledge as to where they would be assigned, or what kind of aircraft I'd be flying.

"I don't know," I confided to Casey. "I thought I'd never wish for another thing when we got our bars, our wings, and then to cap it all off, we got assigned as fighter pilots. Talk about a parlay. I don't feel quite right about even wishing for anything else."

"I know what you mean," said Casey, "but I can't help dreaming about that P-51 Mustang. Talk about a class aircraft. It's got to be the Cadillac of all fighters. Why, the Limey version of the ones we sent them even have Rolls Royce engines in them. It'll be tuxedos instead of flying coveralls next."

I grinned at my partner's fantasy. "I go along with everything you say, Ace. Not only is it the greatest possible fighter to fly combat in, but flying out of England to the Continent to do combat with the

Krauts is at least over dry land. I've never liked over-water missions, even here in the Gulf of Mexico. But in the Pacific Theatre, it's all water, from take-off to return. I'd have joined the Navy if I'd wanted that."

"Yeah," Casey responded soberly. "I sure have a lot of respect for those Navy pilots flying off those flat-tops. Combat anywhere is tough enough. But imagine coming home after a three or four hour mission and having to land on a postage stamp that's bouncing like a yo-yo and you might wish you'd chosen another line of work."

Nodding agreement, I summed it up. "I'll bet a Mustang can cross the English Channel in less than ten minutes. That's my idea of an over-water mission."

John Casey and I and most of the others in our training squadron finally got the word. The overseas orders reflected destinations all over England. The "Junior Birdmen," as we soon would be labeled by the veterans in the fighter groups we would join, were selected apparently at random. Five or six pilots went to each combat group as replacements.

The orders for Lieutenants Abner and Casey were identical: "the 357th Fighter Group, Leiston, England." The 357th flew Mustangs!

In 1944 the *New Amsterdam* was the third largest passenger liner in the world. The *Queen Mary* and the *Normandie* were the leaders. I and a thousand plus other military replacements were aboard her in New York harbor, and soon would be on our way to the European Theatre of Operations, the E.T.O. There were warnings that we might expect one of the heaviest storms so far that year in the North Atlantic. German U-Boats were a constant threat to slower transport ships, but, that September, it was impending storms that had everyone's attention.

Troop movements aboard military transport ships were organized as if the troops being shipped were members of a typical military organization, with a commanding officer, staff, and the usual chain of command found in a squadron or regiment. I was named adjutant of this transport organization in spite of my lack of formal military state experience.

The appearance of their comrade's name and my assignment on the ship's bulletin board caused much hilarity in the ranks of my brother pilot/officers.

"Hey Ab, I knew you were cut out to be a ground-pounder."
..."Look alive, gents. Here comes a real Chair-Bourne Commander."
..."Tensh-hut...Don't salute. Just sit at attention"...and other not so complimentary salutations.

After getting over my initial shock, I found that I was rather secretly pleased with my new assignment. "After all, an adjutant was right near the top of a military table-of-organization. And, this was a real military organization, with a C.O., and Exec., and the whole chain of command," I explained later in my first V-Mail letter home.

I was initiated in my new job before the *New Amsterdam* departed from New York harbor. It developed that a large percentage of the enlisted personnel aboard had been released from military prisons after they had "volunteered" for active combat duty.

"Boy, they are a rough crowd," I informed my pilot buddies in the ship's officer's lounge. "Last night, 12 of them jumped into the bay rather than be shipped out. Imagine, it's got to be a 75- or 100-foot drop from the deck to the water. But, 10 of them were recovered. I don't know if the 2 missing ones made it, or were clobbered by the impact, plus the temperature of the water. Man! It was colder than a well digger's ass up on deck, never name how it must have been in the drink."

This incident was a harbinger of things to come for a young pilot/adjutant. In addition to my more clerical duties as an administrator for the command, I was responsible for the guard rosters which were made up with the naming of the officer of the day, non-coms and enlisted men, whose duties included keeping order and discipline among the rather motley passengers in the lower decks. There were nightly incidents of thievery, fist fights and knife fights, and a variety of confrontations that inevitably emerged from the card games and crap-shoots that went on for 24 hours a day, days on end...The daily morning reports looked more like a police blotter from the toughest city in the world.

During the first couple of days at sea, I felt I was "getting the hang of it, being a desk jockey." This was before the *New Amsterdam* felt the mighty thrust of an angry North Atlantic Ocean.

"Can you believe that, Ab?" John Casey exclaimed. "Why, those seas are higher than this ship. It's got to be over a hundred feet from the bottom of those troughs to the crest of those waves. How in hell do we keep from getting swamped?"

The third largest liner afloat was doggedly plowing into the largest storm so far that year anywhere in the world. The prow of the giant liner dove into the monstrous seas that covered the forward decks with boiling foam, then, shuddering from stem to stern from the force of the icy impact, the ship would recover to do it again. And again. And again, for four days and nights.

One of the duties of the adjutant was to make a nightly grave-yard shift patrol inspection of the various guard watches on the top passenger deck. The duties included the inspection of guard posts stationed along the main corridor running from the rear of the ship to the extreme front, or bow, of the craft. It was here that the narrow bow of the ship caused the corridor to come almost to a point.

Some 50 feet aft of the actual bowsprit, the inspecting officer would open a hatch that led to the outside catwalk, step out onto the narrow walkway, close the hatch, and secure the "dogs" that locked it, and then proceed aft and reenter the next entry way hatch.

The instructions were clear enough in print. It was not physically a difficult procedure to execute...when the weather was good...and the sea calm.

At two o'clock in the morning, in the Mid Atlantic during a storm to end all storms, even the saltiest of veteran sailors would shrink at the prospect. They, undoubtedly, wouldn't risk it.

I, a true landlubber, followed orders.

The rising and falling of the ship's prow, traveling vertically some 75 to 100 feet, caused my knees to buckle on the upswing, and then to almost rise off the deck on the down thrust. It required all of my strength to force the heavy metal bulkhead open into the face of the gale force wind. Then, as I tried to emerge through the narrow opening, the "door" threatened to crush me against the frame.

Finally I was out into the full fury of the tempest. The bulkhead slammed shut of its own accord, and slowly I managed to secure the "dogs" that locked the huge panel, at the same time hanging on with one arm through a stanchion that was welded to the bulkhead beside the hatch. Nearly exhausted, for moments I just hung on for dear life. It was like being on the end of a giant spring board, rising and falling in the deafening darkness filled with howling banshees that tried to tear me from my precarious perch, and fling me into the boiling cauldron.

Later, much like recalling a nightmare, I could vaguely remember going ever so slowly from handhold to handhold, along the narrow, icy walkway, aft to the next exit hatch.

My inspection was finished. And so, almost, was I.

The next day I was questioned by Colonel Adams, the commanding officer, who was mystified by the completeness of my inspection report. The colonel apparently could hardly believe what he saw on the document, and inquired about any problems that might have occurred.

"The weather was pretty bad, sir," I said. "It's probably the worst weather I've ever been in," I continued after a pause. "I'll have to admit I'm not much of a sailor, sir. In fact, I was damned scared. I was wondering if there might be some other way to do it."

The senior officer was not amused. He was horrified! He fully grasped the enormity of the situation.

"You're right, Lieutenant Abner. Until this storm's over, we just won't do it."

"I know it's been over 60 years since my grandad came from the Auld Sod, but it's still kind of a thrill to actually be seeing it," I said. I and a few hundred other Yanks crowded the upper decks of the *New Amsterdam* as she steamed up the Irish Sea that separates Ireland in sight to the west, and England to the east.

The midmorning weather was great compared to the raging storms they had witnessed for nine days while crossing the Atlantic. Already forgotten were the tiered bunks, the cramped overcrowded quarters, and the Dutch breakfasts of "bloaters," fish floating in thin blue milk.

This rather peaceful scene, quiet except for the low excited hum of voices and the muted throb of the great engines below decks, was suddenly shattered by an earsplitting roar. The racket was made by four R.A.F. Spitfire fighters that appeared on the surface of the sea out of the south, and roared over the giant ocean liner bare inches from the top of the ship's funnels.

"Wow! That's what I call a buzz job!" was a comment heard from air jockeys all over the ship.

Again, the "Spits" returned and repeated their aerial welcome to their soon-to-be comrades in the war still being furiously waged on land, on the Continent, and in the skies over Britain. The dramatic appearance of these air warriors had in an instant created a kinship that is found so often between men of diverse origins, joined in combat against a common enemy. This was a welcome indeed.

"My God, those are beautiful airplanes," said John Casey to his mates standing with him watching the show. "Listen to those Merlin engines. Those wooden props are what gives them that strange whine. Boy, they sound and look mean! I'm not sure I'd care to tangle with one, especially at lower altitudes. I'm afraid they'd even give a Mustang a real hairy scrap."

"Amen," I agreed. "You know those pilots have got a lot of aerial combat time. The fact they're still alive proves how good they are after what they've survived. The air battle of Britain was sure as hell no picnic. God, what a job they've done."

"Yeah," responded Casey, "Goering's Luftwaffe really took a beating from these guys. Never have so many been so thoroughly fragged by so few!" he ended, paraphrasing Churchill a little.

The 10-day voyage ended at Gullach, Scotland on the Firth of Clyde below Glasgow. An overnight train ride to Stone, Repple Depot (replacement depot); then, after processing, on to East Anglia, and Lieston, England, where the 357th Fighter Group was putting its name into the history books on aerial warfare. At last, combat!

"Forget about paying your respects to the commanding officer and his lady, lieutenants. In the first place he's probably asleep by now, and he's got a mission in about six hours. And his lady is in Fort Wayne, Indiana. Just sign the book here, and the driver will take you to the B.O.Q. (Bachelor Officers' Quarters) for tonight. Tomorrow, check in with the adjutant at base headquarters and he'll have you processed and you'll get your gear and housing assignments."

The officer of the day said all this, ignored our salutes and pointed toward the door.

Casey and I did as we were told and stopping briefly in the small entry that had been tacked on to the M.P. Quonset, we put on our raincoats and billed hats with the plastic dish covers on them. We picked up our bulging B 4 bags, stepped out into a downpour and waded through a puddle to the muttering jeep that was waiting for us.

"I hope Lieutenant Morse was awake, gentlemen," the driver, a corporal, said. "He's tryin' to catch a nap before he attends the briefing at 0600. I reckon ya'll are goin' to the Biltmore for tonight. I'll get you there in a jiffy if we don't drown on the way."

The "Biltmore" was spartan in its accommodations compared to its hotel namesakes, but we wasted no time in sacking out, and spent the first night with the 357th with a sound that would become familiar. Rain on a tin roof.

We, and four other replacement pilots, spent the next few days getting briefed, drawing equipment, and assignment to quarters. This first week also included a trip to Cambridge, our wing headquarters, where Jimmy Doolittle greeted us and gave us an inspiring briefing that, coming from him, was all we could have wished for.

At last we were assigned to our operational units. I was slated to the 363rd Squadron, Major Carlisle commanding, and to D Flight led by Lieutenant Carter. Casey went to the 362nd commanded by Captain Carlson and to a flight led by John Kirla.

The evening of the day we'd gotten our assignments I met Casey outside his Quonset, and we made our way to the officers' club. We'd been taking our meals at the officers' mess, but neither of us felt like we should enter the "hallowed halls" of the pilots' lounge until we really belonged.

We entered "The Club" with the rattle of a Ping-Pong game in progress, and the clicking of billiard balls from the English snooker tables, all located in a room to our right. On the left was the pilots' lounge, and from there came a subdued roar of voices, laughter and the clinking of glasses. Barely discernible was the background of recorded music playing the day's popular hits.

We casually made our way to the end of the bar where there was a small opening and eventually got a couple of draft beers from one of the very busy bartenders.

Like a couple of sophomore athletes we felt like we'd finally entered the first string's locker room. It was almost impossible not to stare as we tried silently to decide which name belonged to which beribboned Eisenhower battle jacket that clothed the ace within.

By now, we knew the names of the stars of the 357th Group, and we were like typical rookie football players dazzled by an All American Varsity.

Our new group had its share of aces. Captain Bochkay had a dozen victories. He was joined by a number of equally successful combatants such as L. K. Carson who led the group with 19 kills; Bud Anderson, 16; Chuck Yeager with 11, five of which came on one mission; Captain Browning, 7; and Ed Hiro who was shot down in September and whom we'd heard of back in the States, with 5. And there were others, possibly not as glamorous as these names, but all with victories.

"Ah hah! There you are." It was Russ Kalessa, a junior bird-man, J.B., like us, looking like he'd been wearing a uniform all of his life, with a glass of what we learned was gin and tonic, and an air of complete confidence.

"Pretty impressive group, isn't it?" he said with no trace of irony. "I'd give my last buck to know what they have learned. I guess we'll soon find out."

"Hey, you want impressive," I said. "How about Chuck Yeager? The guys in my hut were talking about him last night. He got five victories in one mission not long ago; five 109s, a new record. He had two kills last March when he was shot down on a mission to Poland. He walked out to Switzerland, and when regulations ordered him home, he got Ike to rescind them, and he got back to combat with our group. He was the first to shoot down an ME-262, that new Luftwaffe jet fighter. And how about this? He's led our squadron on some missions, and led the group as a lieutenant. They say he's got eyes like an eagle and can spot a gaggle of Krauts long before anyone else. We've got over 20 aces in this outfit, an he's one of them. I'd like to fly his wing any time."

"Yeah, speaking of flying," Kalessa said. "I talked to a sergeant in personnel today, and he said we'd probably be assigned to Klobber Kollege in a day or so and get checked out in the P-51B, weather permitting. Then a few hours solo in that bird-cage canopy model before we get our own D-Model aircraft."

"And go operational," I added. "Boy, that will be the day."

"Off we go into the wild blue yonder doesn't sound so corny now, does it?" Kal said seriously.

CHAPTER IV *COMBAT READY*

I knew that first night as a bona fide member of a combat fighter group that this was going to be an occasion that would remain in my memory forever. I had actually dreamed of this moment many times during the long months of training. I was amazed at how this actual experience was so different from what I had imagined it would be.

First of all, the atmosphere of this room and its people was unique compared to the scenes depicted in the war movies I had seen. There was no Van Johnson, staring into a glass morosely contemplating his fate. I couldn't find a John Wayne, surrounded by admiring youngsters who obviously regarded him as a god of some sort. These guys were for real.

The area itself was fairly well lit, not the dramatic gloom reminiscent of a Montmartre bistro. And the smoke from dozens of cigarettes didn't hang like a London fog over the heads of raucous extras. Apparently, some enterprising engineer had designed an air conditioner of some sort that actually worked.

The principals in this scene, out of uniform, could have been country club members celebrating the conclusion of a successful home-and-home golf tournament. There was no apparent tension...no brooding and no bravado. Everyone had a glass of some concoction or another, but there were no loud drunks, and no blustering belligerence.

Here and there you could see friendly arguments, with hands raised in the air forming aircraft, the right hand "peeling off" and diving on the left in a deadly attack. Some maneuvers were greeted

48

with laughter, and others gaining nods of agreement. Obviously, pilots can't talk about flying without manual demonstrations.

But two rather incongruous things that also impressed me, that did not concern flying, were sartorial. The first was the "uniform of the day" for the pilots...the Eisenhower jacket. The forest green officer's blouses we were wearing, that we had immediately purchased upon graduation, were definitely passé. Every pilot here, it seemed, had acquired a London-tailored short jacket adorned with a shining square brass buckle at the waist, and of all things, a scarlet lining! Talk about panache. The next absolutely necessary item of apparel was a shining pair of handmade, calf-length boots bearing the label of some "bootmaker for the King" on Jermyn Street. This marvelous made-to-measure footwear resembled short field boots, but were unlike the British Wellingtons favored by the Royal Air Force which were generally fleece lined. These items of the "uniform" worn when on leave or a 48-hour pass, were unique with pilots...like the 50 mission crush, billed officer's hats, and in some cases for officers with a sense of humor, a swagger stick. All marks of the combat warrior.

We three "Jaybees," junior birdmen as we were still labelled, didn't discuss this apparent clothing distinction. But, I know I, and I suspect they, would shed our ground-pounder's blouses and purchase Ike's innovation as soon as we felt qualified to wear them.

Captain Bochkay joined us momentarily to shake hands and welcome us to the "mob," as he called it. And though I would remember his warm attitude and genial remarks, there was another thing unique about his appearance.

"Bock" was not movie star handsome, but he had a craggy face, a jutting jaw, a grin and a rather long muscular neck that all fit together somehow. This neck was wrapped in a shirt collar that was definitely non-reg, a great shade of tan that was a far cry from khaki, and made of some kind of fine linen...and an off-green tie, knotted to perfection that obviously came from a Bond Street haberdashery at the cost of at least a couple of pounds.

I don't know why I was so taken with Bock's "uniform." I guess it was a throwback to my early years and the times I spent in one of my dad's clothing stores. He too was a careful dresser, not a fop, but correct. Maybe I was looking for a substitute father figure.

I discussed this rather odd impression with Case as we waded back to our quarters in the rain.

"No, I didn't notice that," Casey said. "He's sure an impressive guy. Like our new C.O., Lieutenant Colonel Carlisle, he sure looks and acts like an ace...whatever he's wearing. You know, I'll bet he's never been stopped for being out of uniform."

The best way to describe a Quonset hut is to envision a huge steel barrel lying on its side in the mud. As a dwelling it has few redeeming features, but for me it does possess one quality that I personally appreciate. When pelted by a heavy rain or hail stones, it realistically recreates the familiar sound of an Oregon downpour beating on our old barn's tin roof.

The quarters I was assigned to were well located just a few steps from the latrine and shower building. This structure appeared to have been converted from an old dairy barn, though the stalls weren't spacious enough to accommodate even a small cow. This "Ice House" as it was accurately called, had concrete walls that glistened with a frigid sweat, and the slab floor was invariably wet. Two dim light bulbs provided the only warmth in this dank cell, and the showers offered the same cold water as the loo (toilet). The whole atmosphere did not lend itself to loitering, but I suppose it did simulate a Spartan condition appropriate for "valiant warriors."

None of my bunk mates spent a lot of time lounging about in our luxurious quarters. It was rarely warm during the fall, winter and spring months, and most of us spent the evening hours after mess playing Ping-Pong or English snooker in the club, or watching fairly current movies at the base theater. But everyone in our hut was present the first Friday evening that I was quartered there. The reason was the weekly radio broadcast from Berlin Calling that aired about 9:00 P.M.

The highly stylized British voice of Lord Haw Haw came over loud and clear:

"...and I want to extend a warm welcome to the two latest war mongrels to be added to the rosters of the Yoxford Boys, the 357th Fighter Group stationed in Leiston, England. Joining the Anglo-assassins is second lieutenant Alan K. Abner, serial number AO-205-9705, and second lieutenant John Casey, AO-205-8746. The Luftwaffe will be ready for you lads. Don't expect to survive a long tour of duty."

This announcement was greeted by loud hoots and jeers from my comrades, while I, I'm afraid, was sitting there openmouthed.

It soon turned out that my pals had anticipated that this broadcast would follow Haw Haw's weekly practice of such announcements that heralded the arrivals of replacement pilots throughout the 8th Air Force. I joined in the humor of the occasion but still felt a slight qualm at the obvious efficiency of the Nazi intelligence network to penetrate our security. Lord Haw Haw, that renegade Limey bastard, provided a weekly diversion, but I never saw any sign of damage to the morale of the Yoxford Boys.

However, this was not the highlight of the evening nor was it the end of my introduction to Quonset B3. I had been in my sack just a few minutes, when suddenly the silence of our metal cylinder was shattered with two, then a third explosion emanating from the still smouldering potbellied stove located in the middle of the area. Loud, outraged cries, cussing and coughing followed as smoke and ashes floated through the beams of flashlights that came on from various bunks. Numerous men were angrily accused of the dastardly deed, but no one had been seen putting any explosives such as giant firecrackers or three 45 cal. cartridges in the heater, and no one confessed.

Joe Cannon, one of our residents was for a while considered a prime suspect, but he of course vigorously denied any guilt. Later, as I became best buddies with Russ Kalessa, and learned of his penchant for practical jokes, I was half convinced he was the potbellied-stove demolition expert.

The morning of the big day did not dawn bright and clear. In fact, it didn't "dawn" at all. Typically of England in the early fall of 1944, or any other year for that matter, it was dull, drizzly, and gray. The ceiling was under five hundred feet and no mission was scheduled.

But finally, I had a "mission" of my own for this long-awaited day. It seemed that I'd been waiting most of my life for this moment. At last, after months of training, I was ready to "check out" in *the* combat fighter plane of World War II.

"It's supposed to clear up by noon," I said, somewhat anxiously to no one in particular, as I waited in the breakfast chow line.

U.S.A.F.

"I don't know why they don't check a guy out in bad weather, because that's all you're ever going to see in this God-forsaken swamp. You might as well start out in the soup, and get used to it right off." This observation by Lieutenant Carter, my new flight leader, was made without bitterness. Rather, in a sort of laconic tone, he was merely expressing out loud what he and the others around them realized could be true.

"Yeah," another voice chimed in. "Look at last month's casualties in this group. Two lost due to enemy action, and five lost in weather. At least the Krauts, if they have to bail out, are landing in their own territory, and not in the hands of some blood-thirsty civilians, or in the drink."

I listened to this often repeated conversation with half an ear. My mind was totally engrossed in contemplation of what was to happen as soon as the "soup" blew out and I would be cleared for take-off on my first solo flight in the fabled Mustang.

The star of this show was the P-51 Mustang fighter plane. The cast was assembled for the debut performance of ingenue, 2nd Lieutenant Alan Abner, playing in my first support-role. In the background were Lieutenant Carter, my flight leader to be, and my newly assigned crew chief, Percy Blount. And standing by, awaiting its cue, was the P-51 B. The "B" model was no longer combat operational. It still wore the outmoded "Bird Cage" canopy of the early issues. But you had no doubt it was a P-51 Mustang; lean and mean, slick and menacing.

I had previously had one trip in the fighter. That time in a converted B model that had been rigged with a piggy-back seat installed in the place of the removed fuselage fuel tank directly behind the pilot's seat, allowing for an observer passenger. That flight had surpassed anything I had ever experienced, including the 50 hours I had logged solo in the older P-40 Warhawk during transition training. But this now was the Big Time. This was Broadway.

It was true. Getting into a Mustang was like putting on a pair of pants. Though the cockpit was considered "spacious" compared to a Spitfire or the German ME-109, it still touched you on all sides. I went through the Before Starting Check list I had learned to do blindfolded. Finally I was ready. Giving the circling-finger starting signal to Blount and Lieutenant Carter, and getting an all clear, I hit the primer switch and held for the prescribed "3 seconds when cold"; starting switch to "Start," and as the huge prop, 11 feet in diameter, began to turn; mixture Control to Auto Rich. A couple of coughs, a belch of black smoke and the huge 12-cylinder Merlin liquid-cooled engine roared into life. Adjusting the throttle to allow 1300 RPM, I waited for the oil temperature to reach 40°C, and the pressure held steady. When all instruments were in the Green I throttled back to 1000 RPMs and gave Percy the signal to jerk the wheel chocks. Lieutenant Carter gave me a Thumbs Up, a huge grin, and I made my grand entrance into the real world of combat fighters.

Taxiing carefully, I lined up short of the runway, ran up the engine to 2300 RPMs for Mag checks and thoroughly double checked my pre-take off list. At last, on the strip lined up on the center line. Pulling the stick back in order to lock the tail wheel I advanced the throttle smoothly to 35", 45" then 61" of manifold pressure and 3000 RPMs. In the first few seconds of the take off run, my earphones suddenly came alive. "You are cleared to take off Cement 79," droned a bored, but slightly amused Captain "Tilly" Botti, ground controller. I'd forgotten to get take off clearance! The one thing I hadn't practiced for hours on end.

Though momentarily rattled by this omission, I was far too busy to dwell upon it. At maximum take off power I knew instantly why they'd named this roaring charger "Mustang." The British Air Ministry selected the name for their early imports of the P51B-IIIs, by finding Webster's definition suitable: "the small, hardy, half wild horse of Texas and New Mexico." I found this Mustang to be rank and spooky. Untended, the nose came down in the attitude of a bronco getting ready to buck. Too much back pressure in correcting attitude, and too much rudder, and the son-of-a-gun threatened to Sun Fish. This "half-wild horse" required a light rein and plenty of anticipation as to its next unpredictable move.

Finally, three miles farther out and 1,000 feet higher than Standard Operating Procedure, I got the gear up and established a reasonable 500 feet/minute rate of climb. Levelling off at 10,000 ft. I tried a tentative shallow turn. The Mustang responded like a trained show horse. For the first time, I felt like I was in charge.

Cautiously turning, climbing, and diving I thrilled to the performance of this Pegasus. Though flying it required constant attention, its flying characteristics more than proved its widely acclaimed reputation as the world's greatest fighter plane.

"Holy cow! What a machine," I thought with extreme satisfaction. This cowboy would never be the same again. I was hooked. No thrill would ever match this one. A strange union was formed between man and machine. Once you've been there—thrilling and swooping in the clear, thin air—no earth-bound experience would ever come close.

Those first few moments in the fighter proved to me once and for all what my first flight instructor, Mr. Johnson, had told me the day I was to solo for the first time.

"I know you've heard that old expression about 'flyin' by the seat of your pants.' It's usually used in describing how old barnstormers like me fly an airplane. It's not intended to necessarily be complimentary. In fact, I've heard commercial air line drivers say it with a sneer. But let me tell you something. Your rear end could very well be the most sensitive part of your body when you're really flyin' the airplane. If you pay attention and not get locked on your gyros and other instruments, your butt'll tell you the first sign of a skid. You know...when you haven't got enough bank on for the rate of turn your rudder's giving you. And then you can prove it by the needle/ball gyro. It's like a sharp turn in a car. Pressure on your hind end, or the lack of it, plus the sound of your engine will sure indicate you're climbing or diving. What if your artificial horizon isn't working?

And talking about discomfort. Just stick that nose down suddenly when you're in level flight, and your butt comes up off your seat pack and that safety belt starts to cut you in two, and it's about as unnatural a sensation as you want. No sir. When everything else fails and you're trying to dead stick into a corn field you'll be better off if you've got acquainted with the signals that start with your hind end."

I had followed the old pilot's advice throughout my training career, and Mr. Johnson was right.

Before that initial take off in the high-powered fighter there was a lot to remember. I knew about torque, but it had never been like this. Torque was a physics principle that caused an aircraft to rotate on its axis opposite to the rotation of the propeller. When power was first applied, the craft wanted to roll to the left. S.O.P. (Standard Operating Procedure) for any aircraft required putting in various degrees of right rudder trim to compensate for it. If sufficient trim was not entered, a good deal of physical foot pressure on the right rudder could be needed to maintain a level take off.

I had become acquainted with extreme torque in the P-40 Warhawk, but now I apparently hadn't turned in enough trim, and my right leg was almost fully extended before I was airborne and able to reduce power. I wouldn't make that mistake again.

The pressure on my back, caused by the rapid acceleration when the bird quickly gathered speed as it tore down the runway, was about the same as it had been in the Warhawk. I wasn't surprised when the forward thrust pushed me back in my seat nor when my head was pressed against the pad that protected my head from the hard, cold surface of the 3/4 inch armor plate that would guard my back from projectiles from the rear in combat. But I knew I was really beginning to move!

As the plane gathered speed, the tail came up almost without any significant forward stick pressure. Holding it in a level flight position as flying speed increased, the Mustang began to bounce and roll, bounce and roll, and finally with just slight back pressure on the stick, it was airborne.

It's at this point that an experienced "Hot Pilot" will pick up his wheels while still only 8 or 10 feet or so off the runway. It's not entirely showin' off. The quicker the drag, caused by the extended gear, can be reduced, the faster the air speed builds and the sooner you get into the air, increasing altitude and escaping what are the most dangerous seconds spent in flying a high-wing-load fighter.

There is a point during take off when the most experienced pilot in the world can't control his ship. If that massive engine quits, and that 12 foot paddle prop stops, that old devil torque will instantly take over and snap roll to the right into where very unlucky pilots go.

───────────────────────

For some inexplicable reason, for just an instant, the rain pelting the plexi-glass canopy through which I peered down at the darkness, reminded me of an earlier time. A time in another world when I had paused in my milking chores, and looked out of the milkbarn window at the glimmering pre-dawn Oregon countryside. It was the smell that didn't fit. Alfalfa hay and steaming Jerseys created a soft, warm scent that was almost a sedative. Only the rain was the same. The smell of the fighter plane was different. With the bubble canopy "cracked" partly open, the cockpit was permeated with a blend of hi'test gasoline, hot oil, coolant vapors and a kind of ozone-like, static electricity that further charged the air.

The throbbing 12-cylinder Rolls Royce Merlin engine, already pre-flighted and checked meticulously by Crew Chief Percy Blount, rumbled with barely restrained impatience.

"This was it!" For 16 months I had dreamed, struggled, prayed and fought with all of my physical, mental and moral energies for this moment.

"I'd made it, bigod! I was a P-51 Fighter Pilot, in the 'Best Goddamn Squadron in the World,'...and, today I was going to Bremerhaven!"

I was more alive than I'd ever been in my 23 years of living. The excitement of this moment did not have any negative effect on my efficiency. On the contrary, my senses were heightened to such a pitch of intensity that every thought and movement was accelerated as if my actions up to now had been in slow motion. I remembered everything with crystal clarity. Not an item on the check list had been overlooked. When Lieutenant Carter wheeled out of his hardstand next to mine, and Sergeant Blount pulled my wheel chocks, I swung out onto the glistening metal Pierce Planking taxiway, behind my leader, headed for the starting gate.

Kicking rudders, I began making small taxi S-turns in order to keep sight of the plane ahead. The long nose of the P-51 blocked out the view ahead if one taxied in a straight line. The 48 planes in the 357th Fighter Group had been serpentining around the perimeter of the field, taking off in flights of two, and soon it would be their turn. They stopped short of the end of the active runway, halted momentarily and went through their last checklist before takeoff.

The traditionally tranquil English countryside literally throbbed like a roused beehive during these early morning hours of 1944. First it was the "Heavies," the giant bristling B-17 Flying Fortresses, sometimes five hundred or more, taking off and climbing out in the predawn darkness. They crossed out hours before their escort, the fighter groups, followed to catch them before they were over enemy territory. A box of Heavies, containing 30 or 40 bombers, four engines each, all with climbing power on full, sounded to the citizenry below still snug in their beds, like a huge herd of mastodons muttering ominously in the dripping, dark clouds overhead.

Then came the fighters, just as dawn was breaking somewhere, flashing low over the countryside, joining up in flights of four before penetrating the 300 foot ceiling and starting their long climb to get on top at 18 to 20,000 feet. In contrast to their big brothers, the B-17s or B-24s, the smaller planes, high powered single engines emitted an angry, snarling whine, like fighting dogs, lunging on their leashes, straining to get at the throat of their awaiting enemy. There were many ears listening, and many hearts went with the fighters, bent on vengeance for the terror that visited them nightly from above.

Weather. More fighter plane casualties were suffered those days due to weather, than were inflicted by the enemy in combat. As a wingman I was well aware of this, as were all of my fellows. The hours of training under-the-hood of the Link Trainer flight simulator, and many more hours of in-flight formation flying now bore fruit.

The enemy to be aware of now was not human; it was visibility, turbulence, and ice. I concentrated, with almost hypnotic intensity, on my element leader's right wing tip. My own left wing was tucked slightly below, slightly to the rear, and 18 to 20 feet alongside of Lieutenant Carter's. There was little sensation of actual speed as we climbed through the gray cotton-candy mass. We were four platforms drilling through a seemingly endless void with intense concentration...no communication...no idle comment...no thought other than listening for any change in the cadence of our engines, and carefully guarding our position in the formation so that it remained solid and unvarying. Thirty-five minutes to the top.

This was the first time I had experienced actual formation flying in an overcast. Like bailing-out, this kind of flying was much too hazardous to practice in training. It was something that was done when there was an enemy to engage, and when it was the only way to get to him.

I was totally unprepared for the dazzling shock I experienced when we finally broke out on top. The sticky, gray mass we had been engulfed in for so long vanished. Now, a sudden blinding brilliance of a sun a hundred times brighter than I'd ever seen, caused a shock to my senses that caused me to actually cry out in amazement, "Wow! Would you look at that!"

A surrealistic new world lay out before us. For as far as you could see was the white cloud deck...a soft, innocent looking, billowing coverlet that blanketed the ugly earth below. The only signs of life was the appearance here and there, of other flights breaking through, and soon the squadrons of the group were able to join up and establish the course that would unite them with the bombers.

Upon getting clear of the clouds, Lieutenant Carter had loosened up the flight from the death-lock embrace they had maintained during the climb. I immediately assumed the role I was cast to play...constant, scanning surveillance of the entire sky in my range of vision.

"Keep your head moving, Cadet Abner. Get your dome out of the cockpit. 360 degrees. Look alive, stay alive!" I'd had it drummed into me a hundred times by various instructors throughout my training. Now, it was automatic. Look right...high and low, back to the tail. As you come around, glance at the instruments as your gaze goes through the cockpit...cylinder head temperature, RPM, air speed, altimeter, fuel gauge, and on around the circle, past the left wing to the tail. And, repeat. At the same time maintain your formation position to your leader. And really look! That beautiful scenery can change into a deadly arena in a matter of seconds.

I saw Carter look over at me, his new wingman, and he gave me a thumbs-up sign of approval. He'd lost his last wingman three days earlier in a hairy dog-fight over Potsdam. An ME-163, a new German rocket plane, had claimed him.

The ME-163...a manned rocket projectile that blazed up in an almost vertical trajectory to over 30,000 feet, then fell free, with no power remaining, to slash through a bomber formation hoping to clobber an unsuspecting victim during that single attacking pass. Three days earlier, the 363rd Squadron had been escorting as low cover, beneath the bombers, and the rocket pilot, having failed to get a Big Boy in his sights above, nailed Lieutenant Brady as a target of opportunity and total destruction in an instant.

A "floater" is a tiny spot, a slight flaw existing on almost everyone's eyeball, that in the intense brightness of high altitudes can appear to look like a far distant aircraft. As the eyeball moves, so does the "floater," and the impression of movement is uncanny. As a rookie, I damned near called in a "floater" as a "Bogey at 3 o'clock level," but I remembered. Closing one eye, the "Bogey" disappeared, and I was saved the embarrassment that inevitably would follow later during a hazing by my elated team mates.

This day was estimated to be a "Milk Run" for the 363rd Squadron. And it was. Flying top cover for the Bomber Group to the target, the only excitement we experienced was caused by flak that took out two of the Heavies, but burst well below our top cover fighters. The high flying ME-109s did not appear. Radio chatter revealed some action at lower levels between a gaggle of FW-190s, and the 350th Fighter Group. The Americans scored two confirmed victories.

The mission offered enough challenge for me, with the long descent still to make through the ever-present overcast that would still be there on the return to base.

The leg home, with fatigue and weather major factors, was where real pilotage took place. No one, except in an emergency situation, would break radio silence. It was the unwritten "code of the hills." Each flight leader navigated and brought his team home. While still in the overcast letting down, and when he calculated he had crossed the Netherlands' coast line, only then was it standard operating procedure to get a direction steer from the home base, "Earlduke's" radio frequency. As they continued cautiously, descending through the 500-foot altitude level, the leader anxiously sought to distinguish between the gray, raining overcast, and the equally gray

English Channel. Usually, they would break out beneath the clouds at about 250 or 300 feet over the white-capped, turbulent sea. Sometimes, it was lower than that! Sometimes it was damned hairy!

The ground facilities at Leiston Airdrome, the 357th's home base, had a remarkable aviation aid that science had absolutely nothing to do with. The main, active runway ran almost due east and west. And, the landing run was directly in line with an ancient derrick that was located on the channel's beach, exactly three miles to the east. It was really quite a simple landing procedure. All a pilot had to do after a five-hour mission, culminated by a 16,000-foot letdown through the overcast, was to turn right or left when he spotted the breakers on the Channel beach, and proceed to the derrick. A sharp pylon turn to the heading of 270 degrees, and within seconds you were over the end of the runway. Needless to say, every 357th fighter jockey spent as much time as possible when flying "local," to memorize minute landmarks above or below the derrick. A correct turn and heading, right or left, at landfall, with fuel low, could be critical.

I had done my homework on this matter while still flying local in pre-combat Klobber Kollege. But I was still delighted this day that it worked so well under these conditions. The flight was in an echelon right, and there was the runway. Altitude 25 feet, clearing the scrub trees on the edge of the field by a good 10 feet; and it was up, up and away, boys, we're home.

I really greased one in. "Hey, you could land that one on eggs and not crack a shell," I crowed to myself. "Mission number one completed. Only 49 to go." I was vaguely disappointed that we hadn't seen any real action. The muzzles of my six 50-calibre machine guns were still plastered with tape to keep out ground dust. But, I'd done well. Taxiing down the perimeter tract to my hard stand, I rolled back my canopy and gulped the fresh, damp air. It was raining.

There are few sights in aviation as beautiful as a flight of four fighters, coming in at treetop level, at 200 plus miles-per-hour indicated air speed, and executing the 360-degree tactical fighter approach and landing.

The four birds are almost line-abreast...wing tips five or six feet apart, each trailing the plane to his left by another few feet. As the leader crosses the end of the runway, he pulls up sharply, contrails streaming like banners from his wingtips, into an almost vertical, leaning left climb that develops into a sort of tilting loop. At the top of the loop, constantly turning, power reduced, the speed has dissipated rapidly due to the G-force of the climb and the turn. Wheels now extended, and continuing the diving turn, flaps are lowered killing more speed. A good tight pattern will have the aircraft still in a slight turning bank as he comes again over the end of the runway. The wings level out about the same time as his wheels touch down at about 100 m.p.h. in a wheel landing. The leader applies some power at this point, and with wheels rolling, makes a high speed taxi run, clearing the runway behind him for his closely following flight who have duplicated his maneuver. It's beautiful...it's great fun...and the whole thing happens in about 30 seconds.

If you rated fighter pilots throughout the 8th Air Force on a scale of one to one hundred, all of the combat veterans would rank in the 90s. The new replacement pilots who joined the groups included some who had a slight edge in natural ability, but they all were in the 80s, and only needed actual combat experience to quickly reach the peak of their potential. But in every group there were a couple, or three or four, who stood head and shoulders over their peers. In the 357th, Bochkay, Anderson, Johnson, Browning, all aces many times over, were such men. And, of course, Charlie Yeager who was destined to star in the annals of aviation, was already famous for his "eagle-eye" ability to sight and identify enemy aircraft long before anyone else and then to lead the attack.

It soon became evident that another potential "Super Ace" had joined the club. Matt Crawford was one of those rare jocks who were obviously a lot better than other equally trained pilots. He was a natural.

"I just found out who that J.B. was flying local yesterday that I followed up over Norwich." Bochkay was obviously impressed. "His name's Crawford, and bigod, he's in my squadron. I noticed him off by himself practicing Immelmanns in one of the old 'B' models. They were plumb beautiful. I moseyed over a little closer, and I think he saw me, because he dived about 1,500 feet, gaining speed and pulled off one of the most perfect eight-point slow rolls you ever saw. He levelled out, waggled his wings, did a perfect wing over and split-essed into the overcast headed back toward home."

Major Bochkay was not a man of many words. As squadron commander of the 363rd he never bragged of his own considerable aerial exploits, and seldom gave more than a nod or a thumbs-up to other pilots in his command. His comments were really out of character. This guy Crawford must be something.

"You're right, Bock." Captain Browning carefully set his half-full mug of light ale on the pilots' lounge bar. "I saw him shooting landings a couple of days ago, and he executed his pull-up tactical patterns in under thirty seconds, and greased every one on the plank. He can fly, I'll sure agree with that."

Jim Fifield who had joined the group just a few weeks earlier chimed in. "He was a class behind me in flying school at Aloe Field, Texas, and even then, he could beat anyone who challenged him to a mock dog fight. He was always tops in aerial gunnery too. And to make it worse, the guy is a dead ringer for Ronald Coleman."

Bochkay nodded in agreement. "Yeah, I'm not surprised. I checked his 201 file, and he was a collegiate champion pole vaulter, a straight A student, and his military record is full of superior ratings. I'm getting worried about losin' my job."

I was in Transition School at Mobry with Matt, and he was everything they said, and more. He came as close to being "buddies" with Case and me as anyone. But he still retained a sort of privacy that you didn't feel like invading. He was one of a kind. And he could fly like a bird.

CHAPTER V *LONDON UNDER FIRE*

The smoke from my cigarette dissolved almost instantly into the dense fog that smothered the station platform where I huddled with a few civilians awaiting the arrival of the 1540 train that would take me to the city. I had heard that British railways were almost always on time, and that prediction was correct.

It was kind of fun travelling alone for the first time in many months. Up until now the largest city I had ever visited had been Portland, Oregon, and that town would not even be a suburb in this English metropolis of nearly nine million persons. Victoria Station, where we finally terminated, had ten times as many people milling about as we ever get in Newberg, my hometown, even on the Fourth of July. I finally got a taxi and directed the cabby to take me to the American Red Cross, a destination I knew would be reliable though probably pretty dull.

When I arrived it was dark and drizzling, but still fairly early evening, only 1800 or so. My pass didn't go into effect until 8:00 A.M. the next morning as the 357th's custom was to informally release you from their jurisdiction mid-afternoon the day before. This allowed 40 plus hours liberty, but you had no leeway at the end and had to be back on duty by 8:00 A.M. the third day. And no one fooled around with that deadline.

I was assigned a bed in a small room by myself, and after putting on my Class A uniform I went down to the dining room where I was promptly served an austere but welcome meal.

I was sipping a final cup of tea when I was joined by a handsome, well dressed lady with beautifully coiffed grey hair. After asking if she might join me, she provided me with a memory I'll not forget.

She didn't offer her name, and I didn't ask. We talked about my home in the States, my parents and my impressions of her country. No questions about assignment, my duties, or anything that might be military sensitive; rather she talked about London, Canterbury, and other cities that had been ravaged by the air raids, and the inhabitants and their brave resistance to the efforts made by the enemy to demoralize them. In spite of the grim nature of these topics, she was absolutely charming, and left me with a warm feeling of being appreciated as an American ally coming to the aid of her countrymen. When she left, I asked the girl who was waiting on me who she was.

"Oh, that was Lady Astor," she said. "She comes in each evening and visits with you Yanks. She was an American at one time, you know. But for years now she's been in the 'Ouse of Commons in our Parliament 'ere. She's one of us now, isn't she?"

Lady Astor, I learned later, was born Nancy Langhorne in the state of Virginia, and had married an English viscount named Waldorf Astor. Lord Astor, also born in the United States in New York, was returned at an early age to his native country and had been educated at Eton and Oxford. Lady Astor in 1919 was elected as the first woman ever to sit in the House of Commons, and still served in that seat. I had been curious about her accent. I now realized that it was a soft, Virginian drawl influenced by her years in England that had confused me a little at first. But there was no mistaking her sincerity in welcoming me to her adopted homeland. I couldn't have found a better introduction to the land where I would spend the next few months, perhaps years.

I had been briefed by more experienced veterans of the "Battle of Piccadilly Circus" that the American Club was only a few steps away from the Red Cross facility, and I found it with no difficulty through the blackout. It was packed with airmen, mostly Americans, and a few R.A.F. guests, and the "joint was jumpin' " as we used to say. I had a couple of "light ales" as they called their beer, but feeling a little fatigued for the first time since I'd left Leiston, I decided to turn in. It had been a long day, and the change of pace from combat to this relatively calm civilian scene was rather deflating.

The luminous dial on my hack watch showed 23'35 and I was flat on my back on the floor beside my cot. I was vaguely aware of a tremendous explosion that had awakened me, and the building I was in was still creaking and groaning. I got up and went to the window and parted the heavy, blackout drapes. Through the unbroken glass that I noticed was reinforced with a metallic wire mesh, I could see a bright glow from some source nearby.

I could barely see the street three stories below through a thick London fog that was permeated with ashes and small bits of debris that floated down aimlessly. Dim forms of vehicles and people on foot moved rapidly to my right towards the source of the murky illumination.

I opened the drapes wider to allow enough light to enable me to hurriedly dress and to pack my B-4 bag, then made my way down a darkened stairway to the club's entry where a gas lantern cast a flickering glow on the front desk. A girl in Red Cross uniform greeted me calmly.

"Ah, good morning, sir. I see you've been awakened by the bomb. It hit some two blocks from here, but we're in no danger from this old structure toppling. It's been through worse, I wouldn't, however, advise your going out just yet. It's still a bit of chaos just yet. We'll have breakfast ready shortly."

I thanked this unflappable young lady, and with her permission stashed my bag in a small cubicle behind the desk. In spite of her polite warning I knew I had to see first hand what was going on outside. I buttoned up, set my billed cap firmly, and stepped out into a night created by Sir Arthur Conan Doyle.

A pre-dawn breeze was stiffening and the fog swirled and eddied through the canyon between the buildings. I carefully made my way down the street keeping close to the wall bordering the thoroughfare, out of the way of various lorries and ambulances, and personnel leading toward the bomb scene.

I finally reached a vantage point across the street about 150 feet from the huge rubble pile. Home Guard people and those with stretchers and first aid equipment were evacuating survivors from the buildings adjacent to the target area. It was apparent there were no survivors left in the rubble of the destroyed structure.

I was amazed at the lack of noise or confusion. There were occasional loud commands from those in charge of the rescue operations, the rumble of vehicles arriving and departing, but a total absence of any sign of hysteria. The only cries came from babies or youngsters frightened awake into a living nightmare. The rescue efforts were swift and well organized. These veterans of the infamous Blitz launched by Hitler a few months earlier, were well trained in coping with this latest atrocity.

This was my introduction to this "other war" waged on citizenry; on "those who stand and wait"; my first trip to London for "rest and rehabilitation," "R and R" it was called. This night I had met a lady who personified the grace under fire demonstrated by our indomitable allies. And now, I had experienced first hand the nature of the beast we were sent to destroy.

C HAPTER VI *A UTUMN AND W INTER, 1944*

It's been said somewhere by someone, that the three hardest promotions for an officer to acquire during his military career were captain, colonel, and brigadier general.

For me, getting my first gold bars, 2nd lieutenant, had been tough enough for this citizen soldier. Shortly after entering combat, I'd been promoted to 1st lieutenant, and it seemed so unimportant compared to the other challenges I was meeting in the air over Germany every day, that I didn't even mention it in my letters home.

My promotion in rank had not been nearly so significant as my new role in the flight as an element leader. Combat flights were made up of four aircraft; the leader and his wingman, and the element leader and his wingman. When the air battle started, the flight immediately broke up into pairs, the leaders attacking, and the wingmen covering their tails from counterattacks from overhead, the sides, or the rear. This format continued during the fray until the leader had exhausted his ammunition, then their roles reversed, and the wingman became the gun.

I had performed without significant error as a wingman, and finally, initiative and a certain amount of aggressive combat skill as an element leader had resulted in one victory, one "probable," and two enemy aircraft destroyed on the ground.

The operational groups of the 8th Air Force had military personnel who couldn't remember the last time they'd thrown a salute to a superior officer. Commissioned and enlisted men alike meant no disrespect, disregard for regulations or traditional military custom. It just didn't seem to fit the situation in which they lived. Of course, everyone saluted the officer of the day when they first checked in and reported for duty. They saluted the C.O. whenever they met him; a few others on occasion in town, but rarely on the base, and never on the flight line.

All combat personnel, officers, and enlisted people, are truly equals in the waging of aerial warfare. The man who finally pulls the trigger is certainly an expert. So are a multitude of others who are also experts, and who make it possible for the warrior to get into firing position, and who assure, as far as possible, his surviving to do it again, and again. This kind of interdependency, one upon the other, did not require any kind of nonsense in the form of "saluting a superior officer." Forget it!

Anyone who has seen active air duty in wartime knows that master sergeants are the ones who really run the administrative show. Commanders, execs, adjutants, and other titled officers come and go. They are replaced, transferred, promoted, and often killed. The organization must go on, and it's the key noncoms, at all levels, that provide the continuity so necessary for continued operations.

A fighter pilot and his crew chief don't socialize a lot; there's little time for small talk. Rather, "shop talk" would better describe the subject of most of their conversations.

"Boy, she flew like an angel, as usual, Perce," I used to say with variation as I rolled back the canopy. "Sometimes it seems that Merlin engine is an electric clock, running in oil, and kind of drilling us through the air. Wow, talk about fine tuning."

Staff Sergeant Percy Blount had been the crew chief for four different pilots in the 357th. Neither he, nor they, had ever lost an airplane due to mechanical failure. The expression heard in other outfits, "early abort, avoid the rush," had never been in their vocabulary. They delivered.

"That's great, Cap," Blount would respond. "That's super. But one of the reasons, like I've told you before, is you sure as hell don't stress an engine without reason. That's a big part of it."

There was genuine respect existing between us two soldiers. A salute was unthinkable.

A fighter pilot's crew consisted of a number of specialists. The armorer, the person who saw to the installation and maintenance of the 50-calibre machine guns, the bombs, and the auxiliary gasoline drop tanks when required. The radio man provided an absolutely essential element in actual air operations. Reliable communications in a combat or weather situation were truly the difference many times between surviving or "buying it." The people who maintained the oxygen system, the parachute riggers, the fueling services, the quartermaster guys; they all constituted the team that played for keeps.

A 21-gun salute to them would be appropriate.

"Earlduke," was the radio code identification of the control tower at the 357th Fighter Group base. The "voice" of Earlduke was Captain Tilly Botti. When his Mustangs were flying, Tilly was on the horn, whether it was full scale mission, a J.B. checking out in Klobber Kollege, or just some local flying action when it was down-time. His broadcast voice was similar to that of Ed Murrow who was heard nightly on his broadcasts over Armed Forces Radio to the troops, or to CBS listeners back home. The same low key pitch, the same unemotional flat delivery. And, like Murrow, damned effective. He was dubbed "The Mayor of Reno" by the group that had its origins in Tonopah, Nevada. And they'd have voted for Tilly for president.

"He just *sounds* safe," was the way one jock put it. "Always cool and unflappable, and when you heard his voice after a tough day, you knew you had it made."

Twenty-two guns for "Earlduke."

The 363rd had given the Luftwaffe airdrome at Dummer Lake a good pasting. At least 25 Heinkels and ME-210s had been destroyed or damaged in their revetments. Major Bochkay, however, was not entirely satisfied with the manner in which the strafing run had been executed.

"It was not a good run," he explained later to his flight. "The approach run had been too high to begin with, and too long. Ground fire was ready and waiting when our line of Mustangs had appeared over the edge of the field. It was damn lucky we hadn't been blasted out of the sky."

They were damn lucky. The nervous gunners on the ground, having been warned of their approach, apparently were not looking forward with any confidence to the barrage of 50-calibre tracers the fighters would unleash. The German ground forces let go one fast blast, and dove for the revetments.

"Lucky for us," continued Bochkay, "Not a good tactical strafing run. Just pure luck!"

A new acting squadron leader had led this, his first combat mission as commander. Major Bernie Caldwell had been in the E.T.O. and with the 363rd for three months. He'd gone through Klobber Kollege transition to the Mustang, but after two years in the rear seat of a BT-13 Basic Trainer back in Texas, his big problem was unlearning what he *knew*.

To the "Major's" credit, he had persistently pressed his superiors for overseas combat duty until he finally got it. His motives were not entirely stimulated by any great patriotic urge to be a hero. Rather, he was Regular army and the military was to be his lifelong career. He knew that his career would be barren of promotions if he couldn't manage to "get shot at" in combat. But he'd made it. The only problem was his "getting shot at" also included 15 other pilots sharing his military career requirement. And, he hadn't made a good strafing run.

Streaking away from the smoking German airdrome at below treetop level, the 363rd, when clear, started loosely forming up in the typical squadron diamond formation, each member of the flights-of-four closing in on their flight leader. The squadron, climbing now, headed north toward the North Sea intending to fly a half-circle route after crossing out of Germany, over the North Sea, along the Friesen Islands, and across the channel to England and home base. A long haul over water, but one that provided the least chance of encountering flak from ground installations.

The "Major" levelled the squadron's climb out at 10,000 feet. "Holy Christ," I thought, "doesn't he know we're still over the Continent, and a sitting duck for all types of ground fire?" I swore aloud to myself.

The "Major" had decided on this altitude when they'd dropped out of the lower broken overcast that extended from 500 feet to this level, there to be greeted by another layer of clouds some 1,000 feet above them that he knew was solid up to 18,000 feet to the top. Leading the squadron to the top, 30 plus minutes of actual instrument formation flying was not a cheerful prospect. He'd never done it in a BT-13, and on this mission, his first time in command, he didn't relish the prospect. "They'd be over the North Sea in a few more minutes, and they could turn towards home," he rationalized.

The cloud cover beneath them was broken occasionally by "holes" that provided fleeting glimpses of the dark ominous earth below.

Suddenly, one of these "holes" revealed a shoreline, a sizeable city, and a harbor glittering with lights from what appeared to be the whole German fleet! The city was Bremerhaven, a major German naval center, and below was a sizeable portion of the Nazi Navy!

Almost instantly the sky surrounding the "invaders" was full of rocks. Black puffs of low altitude ack-ack exploded in, and around, and below them. Fiery arcs of tracers came from every vessel in the vast bay below.

The squadron formation disintegrated into individual elements as flight leaders broke swiftly up and away, desperately seeking a new altitude and position that would enable them to evade this deadly barrage.

Captain Carter took B Flight up and to the right in a full power climbing turn, firewalling his throttle and prop to a maximum power setting, praying they could scale the thousand feet separating them from the overcast above.

They made it! And, upon entering that solid protective blanket, our flight leader continued to climb, reduced power, and headed northerly in continuous shallow S-turns, hoping to prevent ground radar from getting a fix on our altitude and direction, and then lofting the higher altitude flak heavies into their midst.

Leveling off at 15,000 feet, Carter steadied our course to a heading of 300 degrees when he estimated we were well out of the northern borders of the Continent, and over the North Sea. Cautiously he began a gradual let-down, figuring we would break out of the high cover between 10 and 12,000 feet. He was right. And we did. The undercast was less dense than it had been earlier over Germany, and now we could see a dark, whitecapped, angry North Sea beneath, with scattered clouds skidding across its surface.

"Thank God," I muttered to myself, "our Flight was intact." The "Major" was shot in the ass with luck again! He was intact! His wingman wasn't. Lieutenant Jerry Hite bought it on the first burst. Lieutenant Hagen, flying tail-end Charley in D Flight, also disappeared in a brilliant blast of fire. There were hits on half the members of the 363rd, but luckily we learned later that they were destined to make it back to base with one exception. My Mustang began showing an engine coolant temperature gauge that was fluctuating, showing signs of some damage to the system. If and when it "boiled," 10 minutes of power remained. Then it was a matter of mere seconds 'til the big Merlin engine would freeze solid, and *Daisy Mae* would head earthward. It was in the book.

It's not surprising that operational pilots on the ground talk of little else other than combat and flying situations, when it's "socked in," and the mission has been scrubbed. It's a continuous round of, "then I did," and, "what would you do if?" A favorite topic in almost all of such sessions involves the various techniques of "bailing out" of a wounded bird that was no longer flyable.

The connecting horizontal stabilizer (tail section) between the twin fuselage booms of a P-38 fighter made it almost impossible to exit and still avoid decapitation. The P-40 dropped like a rock, and inclined toward an inverted spin that welded the pilot to his harness in the cockpit. The Mustang, some held, was best evacuated by jettisoning the canopy, rolling it over in inverted flight, trim it nose heavy, and let go! The pilot, it was said, would be catapulted out, clear the tail and fall free.

I held to the inverted theory myself, and now I was going to get the chance to test it.

The coast of Northeast England was estimated to be some 30 or 40 miles away, but was not discernible through the darkening sky, the scudding clouds, and the rain and sleet that now pelted my wind screen. My Merlin engine ground to a halt at about 10,000 feet. Having had plenty of warning for the last 10 minutes, I was ready, and quickly fed in left rudder and nose trim to allow for the plane's gliding altitude, and the sudden cessation of torque that's normally produced by a running engine.

Lieutenant Taylor, my element leader on this mission and number 3 man, moments before had broken radio silence on the Air-Sea Rescue frequency, and gave the May Day, our altitude, course, speed, and present estimated position. Now, as I jettisoned my canopy, and Taylor could see me getting unbuckled and free of all encumbrances in the cockpit, he again called May Day, and updated our position.

At 6,200 feet, I rolled my Mustang over for the last time in a half roll, stopped in inverted flight, released the nose-heavy stick, and was projected out of the fighter like a tumbler coming off a trampoline.

"Son-of-a-bitch. It works like a charm," I thought. The chute opened, as programmed, and I swung suspended in almost silent space. I was alone in a vast, gray stillness. Alone, except for a silhouette that appeared from a couple of miles to the west of my descent. A fighter in a vertical dive...no, in the bottom half of what looked like an inside loop maneuver, in a direct line with my descending course, and starting to pull out at what would become level flight.

Then it dawned on me. It was my own plane! I'd trimmed it perfectly, and it had split-essed on an almost unvarying course, and was now looping back on my falling track.

"Well, if that wouldn't frost your butt," I thought in amazement. "That's one thing they'd never figured on. Getting clobbered by your own airplane!"

The Mustang splashed into the channel some 1,200 feet, and 30 seconds away from me still calling. But in its swan dive, that mighty Mustang had provided one last heart thumping thrill.

The remainder of this bail-out exercise was executed "by the book." The Pilot's Handbook had warned of releasing out of the chute too quickly over water. Procedure said to inflate the Mae West life vest, release the chest clasp, and leg straps of the chute and grasp the shroud straps, and wait until your feet touched the water. Then, let go.

A strong canvas strap was connected from a D ring on the Mae West to an inflatable dingy that was incased in the seat pack of the parachute harness. When I released the harness, and upon hitting the water, the strap to the dingy pulled the rubber raft from its pack, and triggered a CO_2 capsule that inflated the little rubber boat. Then, with the help of the Mae West and the now inflated dingy, I popped to the surface in seven or eight seconds.

As my head emerged, there was the yellow dingy, inflated, and still attached to the strap at my waist. Within seconds I was aboard. I'd been in the icy water less than a minute.

"Son-of-a-gun. Just like in the movies," I thought. I was safe for the moment, but there were things yet to do. Now I felt the numbing cold. The North Sea, and this part of the Channel any time of the year is not exactly a health spa. As the paralyzing chill penetrated my wet flying suit, I hurriedly began the survival ritual. First, put out the canvas sea anchor that would steady the tiny craft in the churning swells, and keep my position intact for the anticipated rescue. Although it was early dusk, the leaden sky and the grey sea created a sullen surface that made putting out the packets of dye to mark the water for spotting airplanes overhead seem useless. But I did it anyway. The three remaining members of B Flight, low on fuel, had circled over me for a few anxious minutes but had reluctantly departed after determining that I had gained the dingy. Now, it was wait for an Air Sea Rescue craft. And hope they could find me in that turbulent torrent.

I later learned what my old mate Case had gone through during all this.

Casey had been grounded this day as it was his "time down," and he'd missed the mission. When the early returns had reported my bail-out, he'd roared at Matt Crawford, and within minutes they were air borne, speeding to the site of the splash-down, to provide air cover and to direct any sea rescue craft to the scene.

They never found me. They circled repeatedly in ever widening spheres over the last reported location. Then they returned to base and then did it again. Finally, darkness nearly complete, and a freezing rain making visibility and staying air borne almost impossible, they were forced to return to base, not knowing the fate of their fallen comrade.

Casey, A Flight, and my crew spent that night in the base radio shack hoping to pick up some word. The storm, raging by this time, had reduced radio reception to a frying and hissing that made all messages, if there were any, unintelligible.

Near dawn, forcing the door open against the howling wind, Casey said he left the smoke and clatter of the communications center, and leaning into a wall of icy rain and wind made his way slowly across the flooded tarmac toward the dim lights now on in the mess hall. Cradling a mug of steaming hot "mud," he said he settled in a secluded corner behind a crackling pot bellied stove and listened to the terrible tympany of the Nor-easter pelting the corrugated roof and sides of the building. Mess halls, machine shops, and hangars all sound the same during a storm. Metal panels, loosened by a thousand gales, clanged and rattled like a whole rhythm section of castanets. Add the booming blasts of the wind and the continuous minute drumbeats of rain projectiles, and it's not hard to imagine a symphony being played by demons.

"God, I hope they find you," Casey said he prayed. "I knew no one could survive a night like this, tossed like a cork in that little rubber boat, awash in that terrible sea.

"What a way to go. I almost wished rather that you'd bought it strafing a locomotive, or instantly, in a burst of flak. At least then it's over quick, and there's no doubt left. God damnit! It would be better to know!"

Instantly, Casey said he regretted his outburst.

"I remember saying, 'Sorry, God. I didn't mean that. We sure need your help tonight, and here I am cussin' and moaning.'"

He said it was the desolate feeling of helplessness, unable to do anything, that was so hard to accommodate. There was no one to fight. Only the elements at this moment to shake your fist at. The implacable storm was an invulnerable adversary. And, usually the victor.

"A lot of questions entered my mind. 'Who's going to tell Lolly? Oh God, I'll have to! The C.O. will write, along with the bundle of his personal things. But, I'll have to write too. What can you say? How can I describe how much he means to me? To all of us."

Slowly, he said, out of his deep depression, the fight in him began to revive. Somewhere, deep down in my gut, a change was taking place. Anguish, and unaccustomed feeling for this combat conditioned warrior, was being overpowered by a more familiar combativeness.

"To hell with this! Ab's not done yet. Until I know, I'm not going to sit around slobbering in my beer. If he's bought it, he's bought it! We've always known the odds. Tomorrow it could be me."

"I hope to Christ it *is* me."

I learned all of this some days later. Case' and I were on a 48-hour pass in London. We'd seen a great show at the Odeon with Sid Fields, and then proceeded to get pleasantly bombed. Finally the pubs closed and we were too far gone to navigate to the Pussy Cat, one of the numerous membership clubs we belonged to, so we decided to spend our last few hours in town in our own room overlooking Piccadilly Circus. It must have been the Johnny Walker red, or the tap water we splashed on it, because it was the only time in all of the months we'd palled around that we ever had a conversation even close to this one. We never had another.

"You know, that Air Sea Rescue crew fished me out of the drink less than 25 minutes after I'd bailed out." I was stage center, and enjoying every minute of it.

The group was grounded for the day. The then brewing storm that had provided the setting for yesterday's events had really blown in full force after midnight, and that day's mission had been scrubbed. Some of the pilots of the 363rd were in the Squadron Ready Room, a fire roaring in the huge sheet-iron trash burner that provided warmth against the damp chill that seeped through the cracks of the rusting Quonset hut. There were expressions of "No shit?", "You're kidding," "You did what?" and "that bird came back at you?" as they listened to me recapping my contest with the North Sea.

Casey, still slightly dazed by the sudden turn of events, sat silently at the back of the room.

"You should have seen those Limey seamen," I continued. "They fished me out of the drink like a goddamn salmon on a gaff. It looked like a PT boat, but they said it was a converted fisher. The next thing I knew I was stripped, put into long johns and some foul-weather gear, and wrapped in blankets. And, then came the good part." I paused dramatically!

"O.K.," yelled Enfield, "then they brought out the broads." The crews hoo hawed delightedly.

I held up one restraining hand in a grand theatrical gesture.

"Not broads, laddies. Something far better than mere pulchritude. It was Demon Rum, mates. And sweeter nectar ne'r crossed me lips. It was hot. It was buttered. It was probably Jamaican. And it was the best goddamn drink I've ever had in me life."

Cheers and applause responded to this announced obvious highlight of my encounter with the North Sea. Little time was spent in explaining or analyzing the fear and anxiety I had experienced. This harrowing happening was, as usual, reduced to the least common denominator possible. The booze was great!

When the "post mortem" was finally exhausted, Case and I drove off in a jeep toward the flight line to pick out a new Mustang from the group's "remuda" to replace the one I had dunked.

"I hope we can find one that doesn't know how to do a perfect loop," Casey said seriously.

I nodded gravely.

Leiston, England

Dear Don,

I should say "Dear Doctor," because I've got a little problem, Doc, and as usual I come to you for advice.

It's really funny. All through flying school, and now in combat, *I've never been scared.* I mean it. Of course, unless you're entirely stupid you sure as hell are concerned when the mission of the day turns out to be somewhere like Schweinfurt or Potsdam. But you immediately start planning and you just don't have time to be *scared.*

When actual combat starts and you're in a hairy dog fight you're just too damn busy to feel anything except maybe anger and the drive to clobber your opponent. It's a little like a dead serious boxing match, only the end result is quite a bit different.

The only signs I see of real fear in the guys I fly with are those that have only one or two missions left to fly to finish their tour. We've had a couple of them dive in a jug the night before their last mission. But that's rare. There were a couple of Junior Birdman hot shot replacements that strutted around the club when they joined us, wearing white scarfs with their Eisenhower jackets for Christ's sake.

They both turned back and taxied in from the end of the runway on their first mission. But boy. They were an exception. And they weren't here the next day.

But damnit. It seems unnatural that I don't feel something. The only thing that leads me to believe I'm reacting in a funny way (shade of Psych I) is what happens once in a while just before I go to sleep. As you well know I sleep on my back (yeah, and snore) and just before I go to sleep I feel like I've turned to stone. My whole body feels like it's made of concrete and I couldn't lift an arm or a leg if I had to because of the weight. It's not real terrifying, but it sure is unusual. And I always go to sleep. I don't even dream much. No nightmares.

Well, Doc. I'd be interested to know if you get scared (I'll be surprised if you do), or if you too are trying to be a petrified man.

Good luck,

Alan

The United Service Organization (U.S.O.) was made up of volunteer actors and entertainers from Hollywood and Broadway, and they accomplished almost impossible things in order to entertain American troops on active duty around the world. They performed in all kinds of weather in the jungles, on the beaches, anywhere they could pitch a tent or acquire a shelter in which to put on a show. The U.S.O. unit assigned to England had it relatively simple. Every town and hamlet had a theatre or hall where travelling troupes had performed many times for centuries.

Ipswich, the county seat of Suffolk County in East Anglia, was located a few short miles from the English Channel, and due to a fine harbor was an important historic seaport. One of the less imposing structures in this old city of churches, schools, and museums, was the rather modest hostelry known as the Nordic Arms Hotel. It had been named, it was said, in memory of the Vikings who had invaded the area in 991 A.D. There was little evidence remaining of that ancient incident in the decor of the Nordic Arms, but what was more important than antiquity at the moment was the availability of a ballroom-theatre-meeting room space that would do nicely for a party for the pilots stationed at nearby Leiston Airdrome.

The local U.S.O. unit recruited a group of local ladies who, without much persuasion, planned and prepared a "Pursuit Pilots Night" in honor of the 357th Group stationed some 20 odd miles away. The pilots, to a man, accepted the invitation with enthusiasm.

The motor pool of the 357th had the usual assortment of ground vehicles to be found on any American military base. The selection of trucks, in addition to the all purpose jeeps, was said to have been described by a rather unsophisticated airman when asked what he had available in stock as, "We got 2 by 2's. We got 4 by 4's. We got 8 by 8's. And we got them big 'Mothers' what go Choo!"

Casey and I and a "gaggle" of our comrades were crammed into one of those big "Mothers" and took off on our "Night Mission" to Ipswich. It was still two hours until dark when we left the home base, and proceeded down the glistening two-lane highway, winding its way through the rain-soaked, sodden countryside.

"You might as well quit cussin' the weather," said Lieutenant Crawford. "If it wasn't for this storm, we'd be flying a mission tomorrow, and this party tonight couldn't happen."

"How about that," responded the always taciturn Lieutenant Enfield. "Our comedian has turned into a philosopher. Every cloud has a silver lining. Unless it's filled with flak."

These words, as if they were designed to forecast what happened next, were dramatically punctuated by a terrific blast that almost overturned the heavily laden truck.

As we quickly ground to a halt, there was a loud confusion of yells and exclamations. "What in hell was that? We hit a land mine; somebody dropped a bomb!"

The last comment came closest to being the most accurate.

The truck quickly emptied, and as our rather stunned group of pilots, unused to ground warfare, surveyed the surrounding terrain, it became apparent what had happened.

A column of smoke rising from a knoll some two to three hundred yards from where they stood, indicated a sizeable explosion had taken place. A huge oak tree near the impact area, shredded of its leaves, its naked boughs still trembling, stood like a skeletal witness to the presence of the enemy. "It was Buzz Bomb," said Casey. "The damn thing must have malfunctioned, and it fell short of its target on its way to London."

People were now emerging from a large, gray farmhouse that was situated another few hundred yards away. From where the Yanks stood they could see the black holes left where windows had been. Pieces of the roof were torn away, and just a few bricks remained where the chimney had been. A slight hill stood between the dwelling and the site where the bomb had hit, providing a little vertical deflection of the ground blast, otherwise it's doubtful the structure would have survived.

There wasn't a leaf remaining on any tree or shrub within range of their view. The very terrain seemed in a state of suspended animation, and an eerie silence pervaded the entire area.

"Wow! Now you know what one of those babies can do when they land in London," said Crawford. "They take out a whole city block, and everyone in it."

The local Home Defense people soon began to arrive upon the scene, and when it became apparent that luckily no one had been injured or needed their help, we, now subdued pilots, climbed back into our transport and proceeded toward our "night on the town."

It took some doing for most of us to get back into a mood for revelry. Aerial combat was one thing, where it was all rather neat, clean, and if the worst happened, usually over in an instant. But this was different. Suddenly and graphically, we had a brief glimpse of what being a civilian was like on the ground. More than one fighter jock thanked his stars he hadn't been assigned to the infantry. And they would have agreed unanimously that living or fighting on the ground in this war had serious disadvantages.

Ipswich, like all English cities during this wartime period, was in deep blackout by the time we arrived. The nearly hundred thousand souls in the town were snug indoors sheltered from the storm that roared out of the North Sea. The only structure identifiable as they slowly made their way through the narrow streets was the Tudor roof of St. Margaret's. Though an important seaport, Ipswich was spared the nightly bombing that rained down upon London. And though the inhabitants were scrupulously careful about revealing any exterior lights, this did not prevent them this night from creating a cheerful atmosphere indoors for their Yank guests.

The gloom created by our earlier Buzz Bomb experience was soon dispelled by the warm welcome that greeted us as we arrived at the small hotel where the modest ballroom had been decorated for the occasion.

A gracious, well coiffed, grey-haired matron headed the reception line that greeted the group, and spoke a few words of welcome to the visitors. Shedding our parkas and short coats, we Yanks quickly began to mingle and "shop" for a partner for the evening. A few of the airmen, including me, headed for the bar that was located in a darkened corner of the large room. There, each visitor deposited his contribution of a bottle of his liquor ration, and two competent barmen, now stocked with an inventory they hadn't seen in years, did the honors.

Grandad Bowler was known to take a nip or two upon occasion. Occasions were not only those times that were designated as holidays, like New Year's Eve, Fourth of July, Saint Patrick's Day, and others. An "occasion" occurred every Saturday night for him. In his younger "Cowpoke Days," a Saturday night in town was a total failure if you didn't get roaring drunk and had a fight. He had mellowed a little as he grew older, but he still paid his dues at the local Elks Club, and he was a regular there at week's end for a "wee drop or two" and a few games of English snooker. He would invariably win a few drinks playing expertly at this game early in the evening. But as the night and the nips progressed, his eye and his touch diminished so that his bar tab evened out in the end. At home at the ranch Grandad still presided over the Yuletide egg-nogs, and he judiciously prepared any punch that was served on other festive occasions. These relatively mild concoctions and an occasional beer were the only spirits I had ever experienced, until I became a combat pilot, and "fell in with evil companions" during 48-hour passes to London town.

At first, Scotch whiskey was awful! "It tastes like quinine mixed with sulphur and molasses," was the way I described my first taste of Johnny Walker's pride. "It must be good for you, because it sure tastes like hell." But I found it was true, that a liking for Scotch was an acquired taste, as I'd been told by older, wiser, and more experienced jocks. I had learned to enjoy it, and to my surprise, found that I had a rather unusual capacity. I was told I never looked, acted or sounded intoxicated. And I never lost control. Casey said, "You had to know Ab to recognize the telltale beatific smile that adorned his Gaelic countenance when he was 'in his cups.' " It was during these times I think that I most strongly resembled my grandad.

My warm reveries as I sat at the end of the bar watching the dancers, and listening to the local band was pleasantly interrupted.

"I was thinkin' you might be a chaplain or a chaperon of some kind. But then, I noticed you enjoy a glass, or two, or three, and I guessed you perhaps didn't know how to dance. You're not recovering from a near fatal wound, I hope?"

The speaker was in uniform. But I quickly forgot that, because crowning the disguise was the face of Merle Oberon.

Rising steadily to my feet, I looked down at the Wren standing before me, and put out my hand.

"I was about to say 'howdy podner' but it seems that 'good evening, ma'am' is more proper. You surely do brighten up this place."

Radar Specialist Cynthia Roberts, as her name proved to be, flushed a little at the compliment.

"Well, thank you, sir," she said, emphasizing the "sir." "Seeing as you outrank me considerably, as a mere sergeant, I hesitated to invade the privacy you are obviously enjoying. If I was any more brazen, I probably would even accept a sip of whatever it is that seems to benefit you so greatly."

And so "the ice was broken," as they say. Typical of English bars in the whole United Kingdom, it was the only ice in evidence, and it quickly disappeared.

Conversation flowed easily between two off-duty soldiers. Little time was wasted in small talk, and getting acquainted. I was pleased but not really surprised that Cynthia had also come from a rural background. Her father's dairy farm was not far from where we sat, and an eavesdropper would have been startled to overhear a Yank's "line," while talking to a pretty girl, concerned an account of his difficulty in getting rid of the smell of fresh milk from his hands, even his clothes, when preparing to go out on a date.

Our conversation was mixed with much laughter and subdued chuckling. But between anecdotes, our eyes would meet, and the warm camaraderie that had marked their first contact was slowly replaced by deeper, more meaningful expressions.

"You know who I thought of when I first saw you?" I asked. "Merle Oberon. Have you ever seen Merle Oberon in the movies?"

"Of course I've seen her in the movies," the girl responded tartly. "And you're absolutely correct, Captain. I'm a dead ringer for her. It's just that I haven't the proper political connections, or I'd be a star on the movie screen instead of a sergeant looking at a radar screen."

Delighted at the deft manner with which she had covered her concealed pleasure at this compliment, I was enchanted that I had found a companion that so easily matched my own personality. "Ah," I thought. "The luck of the Irish. Or maybe it's the Welsh."

The time passed so swiftly that I was startled when the band, obviously well versed in the traditions of their Yank audience, began the familiar strains of "Goodnight Ladies."

"Holy cow. Is it that late already," I exclaimed. "And I haven't asked you for one dance. Look, I'm not much for jitterbugging, but I can manage this, I think. What do you say?"

It soon became apparent to me, that not only did Cynthia look a lot like Merle Oberon, but inside that heavy, wool, blanket-weight Wren uniform lived a slender, svelte, graceful Merle Oberon.

There was nothing fancy about this last dance. No twirling or dipping. Just two war weary people caught up for the moment in a tender pause in their hectic careers, closely wrapped in each other's arms as they turned and swayed slowly to the cadence of the old, familiar, bitter sweet ballad. Our kiss as the final strains faded was for us the most natural ending to this part of a perfect evening. And it also held the promise of things to come.

Ipswich, like any other English town at night during the World War II blackout was a maze not to be easily navigated when carrying a load of Johnny Walker Red Label, unless you had a guide. Cyn', as I now called her after three hours getting acquainted and sipping on Scottish dew, was an unerring homing pigeon. Huddled under the "brolly" she provided, we wound our way through puddled streets and alleys to "her place," as she described it. It was a snug little dwelling located at the rear of a larger estate. It had been a carriage house in better days, and now was converted to a rental unit by the owner.

There were a few embers still smoldering in the tiny coal burning fireplace, and Cyn' quickly had it glowing with added fuel from her precious reserve. A teakettle was soon whistling on the electric plate, and hot toddies quickly dispelled the chill we'd acquired during the short walk through the still raging storm.

The change in her was almost magic. Looking up from where I sat in a deep chair by the fire, I could hardly believe my eyes. She had only been gone from the room for a few minutes, but in that brief time, an almost eerie transformation had taken place. Gone was the shapeless, lumpy uniform that leveled and squared the feminine form that existed within. Now wrapped in the soft folds of a dressing gown, the soldier disappeared and a lovely young woman emerged. But what was most startling was her hair. So fascinated had I been with her exquisite facial features, that I hadn't even noticed the chaste bun that rode on the nape of her neck, appropriately in style with her military apparel. Now, the braids were loosened, and her long, brown, luxuriant hair fell softly upon her shoulders.

"Migod," I exclaimed I'm afraid breathlessly. "You've got to be the prettiest thing I've ever seen. I'm almost afraid to touch you for fear you'll disappear."

But she was for real. And time and the war briefly ceased to exist for these two refugees from the storm that still raged over this small English town, and over most of the world of 1944.

"It really was a great night," I said, descending to my bunk mates the events of my evening in Ipswich. Carefully omitting the romantic details of my amorous adventure as befitted an "officer and gentleman," I devoted most of my account to finding my way back to the hotel site after many wrong turns and detours.

"The trucks had been gone over an hour," I recalled. "I figured if I got out of town and on the main road north to Leiston, I might get a lift home. If not, it was 24 miles to the base, and walking at a military pace, I could make it in six hours."

There was no traffic on the road that night. I arrived on foot at the main gate of the 357th F.G. at 8:30 A.M. It was still dark, and still raining. I felt fine.

Lucky for Flight Officer Chester Wilmot, his first combat mission would be a "Milk Run." That would be the only luck he would have that day. There would be no advance warning for the series of mishaps that would overtake him on his maiden effort with the 357th Fighter Group. He'd gotten through Klobber Kollege transition all right, and his indoctrination and introduction to the P-51 had gone well. He'd learned quickly how much he had to learn.

Five flights locally, and some 15 hours flying time in the P-51B, and Wilmot figured he was really getting the hang of it. He'd engaged in a half dozen mock Dog Fights with other J.B.s who were also getting checked out in the fighters. And, he hadn't done too badly. Nothing to get cocky about, but he'd done O.K. That is, until he tangled with Bochkay.

Major Donald Bochkay, C.O. of the 363rd Fighter Squadron, was checking out a new Merlin engine on his bird, that, with him, had scored nine kills. The weather that morning had grounded the entire 8th Air Force. But, by mid afternoon, there was a break in the skies, and the sun even showed through the few remnant clouds. Major "Bock" happily took to the air and put the new V-12 through its paces. For half an hour he left contrails all over the moisture-laden atmosphere of Norfolk County which lay north of his home base at Leiston.

Finally, satisfied with his new power plant, he turned leisurely toward home at about 3,500 feet of altitude when he was spotted by F.O. Wilmot cruising in his P-51B.

Wilmot did not "attack" his squadron leader. Rather, he drew even with him at a distance of about 100 yards, and waggled his wings in a friendly manner. "Bock," recognizing his new club member, likewise waggled back, and motioned the young recruit to move in on his wing.

The fledgling was delighted when the major, using the sign language that all pilots communicate best with, indicated it O.K. for Wilmot to get on his tail, and they'd have a little simulated dog fight.

"Hey, this is great!" thought Wilmot, as his "target" started on an easy climbing turn, with him some 80 to 100 feet behind "in trail." They stayed in the turn that gradually tightened as the climbing attitude became steeper. Soon Wilmot became aware that it was becoming more difficult to keep his nose slightly ahead of his "enemy" in a firing attitude. Finally, he was using all of his flying skills to just hold his position.

Suddenly, in the bat of an eye, Major Bochkay was gone! Frantically the young pilot wheeled his plane up and over and searched the skies in all directions, but no aircraft was in sight. "Where in hell has he gone?" was the forlorn question he asked, that was answered later when he met the major in the Ready Room.

"It usually happens a lot faster than that," Bock explained. "When someone's on your tail, and you know you can't out-dive him, and you're in a turn, try to keep him from getting his sights ahead of you for a deflection shot. Climb, and turn tight enough to keep him from getting inside of your turn. Hold it as long as you can. Then, here's the gig. If you're turning to the left like we were, as hard and as fast as you're able, drive the stick as far forward and to the right as you can...And, at the exact same time, hit full right rudder."

The young pilot was all ears. But it was his eyes that bulged slightly when the full implications of what he was hearing began to sink in. He knew about negative G forces. He had heard of the perils of inverted spins. Just visualizing what this maneuver would do to both the pilot and the aircraft was enough to make one's head ache.

"It's a little rough all right," said Bochkay as he watched his young charge's reaction. "But not as rough as the alternative...getting your ass shot off!"

Wilmot's dog fight with Major Bochkay had taken place some weeks before. Now, Klobber Kollege was behind him, and the day he had long awaited was upon him. Today was the big day. Wilmot was flying his first combat mission with the 363rd Fighter Squadron.

So far, the whole morning was going O.K. The briefing indicated the mission was not expected to be too rough. The weather at home was good for England, and a nice escape opportunity was predicted inland, over the Continent, with the existence of a friendly overcast, 2,000 feet thick, with the top at 12,000 feet.

An early fog had blown off with a 15 mile per hour wind out of the northeast. Wilmot was Number 4 in D Flight, "Tail End Charlie," thought Wilmot... But, what the hell. He'd make it. He was a combat fighter pilot.

The last two planes in the squadron, Red Flight, piloted by Element Leader Aaron and his wingman Wilmot, made their last taxi turn into position on the runway for takeoff.

The flagman-starter stood, legs apart, on the edge of the runway, even, and facing the two aircraft waiting to be waved off.

"What in hell is he doing?" Wilmot looked with mounting confusion as the starter, his arms extended in front of him, moved them in an up and down scissoring motion. Repeating this a number of times, he finally waved wildly at the waiting wingman.

Wilmot was getting really rattled. "That's for flaps down, isn't it," he muttered. "Well, dammit, they're down. 15 degrees. That's right. What's he want anyway?"

Precious seconds ticked by. The squadron was gone, and here they sat. The starter, in desperation finally ran out to the Mustang and crawled up on the right wing. Wilmot, rolling the canopy back, heard the now enraged signal man scream, "Open your goddamn oil shutters, you idiot."

"Oh my God," the wingman groaned, quickly making the adjustment. "What a stupid mistake."

Finally, the two last members of the 363rd were airborne, and "joined up" with the other two members of their flight.

Element Leader Aaron noticed his new wingman seemed to be having trouble keeping up with the climbing formation. Turning his head further back to get a better look at the plane to the rear and off his right wing, he noticed that Wilmot's flaps, set at 15 degrees take off setting, were still down.

"Red 3 to Red 4...pull up your flaps," said the voice in Wilmot's ears.

"Oh jeeze," Wilmot groaned, still slightly numb mentally from his earlier error. He'd goofed again! Quickly he reached down and pulled up the flap handle. They came up, all right! Then, with the drag created by the down positioned flaps released, the Mustang leaped ahead out in front of the flight.

Finally, the now thoroughly shaken youngster pulled himself together enough to begin to function as he'd been trained. Slowing his aircraft, he regained his correct position on his leader.

"Holy Toledo...if I'd done that in flying school, I'd have been washed out," he said to himself. "Aaron must think I'm a real jerk."

The 357th Fighter Group took up its escort positions with the bombers, and each squadron was now crisscrossing. The 363rd Squadron was high above, the 362nd below the bombers, and the 364th was even with the lumbering B-17's of the 55th Bomber Group. The 363rd in its "top cover" position saw no Luftwaffe fighters in evidence.

Suddenly, as they neared the "I.P.", Initial Point for the turn to the bombing run to the target below, the lead bomber released the black smoke column that designated the exact point each bomber would use to make its turn, and allow each bombardier to make his run to the position where his plane's bombs would be released.

It had happened before. A new fighter pilot on his first mission was all eyes and ears...doubly alert, determined to do well, with all of his senses highly keyed in this fantastically new situation, where unknown dangers could appear at any instant...head turning constantly, sweeping the skies fore and aft, alert for any surprise attack from an enemy aloft. Wilmot was a new combat fighter pilot.

Suddenly, there it was! A huge blob of black smoke at 10 o'clock low, just under the leading bombers!

Hit the transmitter button!

"Flak...Flak...10 o'clock low,...Break, Break!"

Other rookie combat pilots had done it before. This time it was Flight Officer Wilmot, Red Four of the 363rd Fighter Squadron, flying top cover..."Tail End Charlie."

The squadron momentarily shuddered as they reacted to the alarm. Various flights of the 363rd broke up and away from their positions to get away from the dreaded announced flak.

"Scratch that," came the voice of Squadron Commander Bochkay. "That's the I.P. signal. Rejoin and maintain formation."

For Wilmot, it had not been a very good day.

There was no hazing of the unfortunate rookie that night in the club. No one mentioned the incidents, three of them, that had marked the performance of their newest member that day. Neither was he "chilled" by his comrades. It was down-time as usual. Hoist a few at the bar, maybe a game of snooker or Ping-Pong, chow down, and go to bed. Tomorrow is another day.

Dinner at mess that evening featured an entree that was "affectionately" known as S and S, or shit on a shingle. It was a grey, muddy, sticky concoction that appeared quite regularly on the chef's menu. It was not a recipe you really hated, nor one you just couldn't eat. Rather, it was something that looked pretty bad, but was said to be nourishing! Wilmot, like the others, presented his tray to the server in the chow line, and a generous portion of S and S was splashed on the piece of toast that received it.

Flight Officer Wilmot was in a sort of daze. The day's events formed a kaleidoscope in his mind. It seemed as if he had dreamed the whole thing. As was the custom of the 357th, everyone dressed for dinner...Class A's...pink, *elastique* pants; green Eisenhower jacket with its red satin lining; tan shirt with a green tie, or a green shirt with a tan tie; the works. But the fresh clothing did little to lighten the gloomy visage of the forlorn "rookie."

Carrying his steaming tray, Wilmot proceeded to a place at the long picnic tables and benches where others were already seated. As he turned and swung his leg over the bench to take his place at the table, the S and S loaded plate skidded off its pad, did a perfect inverted loop, and belly flopped onto Wilmot's lap.

Dead silence fell upon the entire table that moments before had held the usual chatter and banter that accompanied the evening meal. The featured player of this scene stared down at the catastrophe that covered him.

Slowly he looked up, raised his eyes to the ceiling, and stated in a quiet, measured tone: "I'm going to hit the sack before I do something else to kill myself."

When he crashed, 1st Lieutenant Chester Wilmot was credited with 3 confirmed victories, 2 probables, and 3 damaged enemy aircraft.

Chet Wilmot didn't do anything wrong that caused his death. He was an excellent pilot, cool and competent in the worst of weather, and skillful enough in combat that no enemy pilot had ever come close to clobbering him.

No, it could have happened to the best pilot in the E.T.O. On his thirtieth mission, carrying a full combat load, he lost his engine on take off. It happened in an instant. Barely 50 feet off the ground his Merlin engine failed, his prop ground to a halt, a lethal pirouette and he "bought it," a bare hundred yards off the end of the runway.

Wilmot was toasted by his comrades that night in the pilots' lounge. His "Fifty Mission Crush" officer's cap was added to the row of others behind the bar. His wingman, as was the custom, was attired in his leader's A-2 jacket adorned with the skull and crossed swords squadron emblem that was bravely displayed on the front. Wingman 2nd Lieutenant Davis wore his inheritance, this worn leather mantle, with pride, and a lump in his throat.

Dear Don,

The last time I wrote I think I told you about not being scared, and that I was beginning to wonder if I had all my marbles. Well, you may be relieved to learn that I'm O.K. I've recently been scared alright, and it wasn't a pleasant experience. It happened in a way I never anticipated and I had no pre-plan worked out in my head.

I was flying Captain Carter's wing in D Flight on this mission, and the 363rd Squadron was assigned top cover at some 28,000 plus feet over the bombers. The target was Chemnitz, a city southeast of Leipzig, and we were about ten minutes from the bomb drop when it happened.

The weather was lousy over most of Europe with towering cumulus rising to the 30,000 foot level, with cloud caverns between the monstrous white structures that provided occasional glimpses of the brown earth far below. There was also a broken undercast at about 8,000 feet, a factor that was going to soon be important. We hadn't been alerted from other groups of any Luftwaffe fighters in our area, and the mission so far had been without incident though we knew there would be plenty of flak and probably enemy aircraft at the target.

I was doing my usual chores at my position off Carter's right wing, my head constantly turning, scanning the skies overhead and from nose to tail, on the alert for any enemy threat. I certainly wasn't bored with this routine; as usual my efforts intensified as we neared the danger zone. I had turned my head to the right to clear the area above and to the rear of our course and used the few seconds or so that scan required. As my gaze came back through the cockpit to check my formation position, I couldn't believe my eyes. Carter was gone!

I know I must have screamed as I pressed the intercom button on my radio. "Cement Leader, where's Red One?"

"He just peeled off, Red Two," Bochkay's voice answered.

I immediately did a half roll to the right, and when inverted, split-essed going down at full throttle into a canyon between the towering clouds, looking frantically for my leader's Mustang that had approximately a 15 or 20 second head start. If he was diving at 300 to 350 mph as I was he had to be at least 15,000 feet below already. I was close to panic.

Where in hell was he? Why hadn't he radioed he was cutting out? He must have seen some bandits and attacked. Where were they? What direction would they have been going? They must have been heading south in an opposite heading from our course.

I was rapidly approaching the undercast at 8,000 feet and had to throttle back and slow my descent down. I leveled off on top of the lower cloud cover and rapidly looked in all directions. No bandits. No Carter.

I continued on in a southerly direction making wide shallow S-turns, but no luck.

Finally, I did a 180-degree turn, reversing my direction and started a climb back on the course my squadron had been taking, thinking I might catch up with them. I switched my radio to C Channel, Emergency Ripsaw.

"Ripsaw, this is Cement 79. I'm separated from my group. Can you give me a steer to rejoin? Over."

I hated to break radio silence but I needed a little assistance.

"Cement 79. Suggest you join any friendly group you can locate. Out." Ripsaw was terse and of course correct.

I had continued climbing and zigzagging through the passes between the mountainous cloud structures, northernly in the general direction of our previous course. But I soon realized the bombers and our guys had long since reached the target and by now were headed for home. I had yet to see any aircraft, friendly or enemy.

I knew I could never catch up. I was on my own, deep in Germany and miles from allied territory. My only chance was to get the hell out of there!

Uncaging and adjusting my gyros, I took up a heading of 264 degrees, the "average course home" that had been given at the pre-mission briefing, and dodging the towering cumulo-nimbus build-ups with their vicious up drafts, I threaded my way up cautiously, and broke out on top at 28,000 feet.

The blinding sun was on my left at about 185 degrees as the briefing officer had predicted and from him I had also learned that the wind at this altitude would be almost due north at 90 mph. I had plenty of gas, my oxygen feed was working perfectly, and so far, no enemy was in sight. I continued to climb at 500 feet per minute, and when the controls got a little mushy I levelled out at 36,000 feet, trimmed straight and level at cruise power settings, and I was solo at the top of the world.

I have never minded being alone, but this was ridiculous. At the same time, I have never been so aware of how insignificant I was. There was no feeling of speed or any kind of movement except the gentle vibration of the engine. It was like being in a cosmic vacuum where humans didn't exist. I didn't pray. I was kind of out of practice. But I did recall what Mom had said in one of her letters. About "not a sparrow shall fall..." or something like that from her prayer book. I didn't feel the need for any divine guidance. Somehow I never doubted I would make it.

Daisy Mae performed like the thoroughbred she was, and I saw no aircraft, enemy or otherwise. Finally the soaring cloud monsters were behind me, and through the now somewhat broken overcast far below I made out what looked like the Rhine River, and I knew I was nearing friendly territory. I began my descent and when I reached 5,000 feet I was able to detect and identify Antwerp as I approached the channel which, as usual was covered with a solid strata layer that I could see extended far to the west toward England and home.

I didn't need to radio Earlduke for a compass steer to R 85 as I was well oriented. I was still feeling a little guilty about breaking radio silence when I called Ripsaw earlier. I got under the cloud cover over the Channel at about 300 feet, and as I approached the beach I soon picked up that lovely derrick and made my final turn to approach our airdrome at Leiston.

The most beautiful "voice" in the world, that of Tilly Botti cleared me for landing, and I even managed to grease one on the runway. I was the last plane of our group to return that day.

Percy, my crew chief, didn't ask any questions when he helped me unbuckle and dismount. He could see my 50 calibres hadn't been fired, and he must have been curious as to where in hell I'd been, but he really didn't want to know.

It was then I began to sweat. It was then that I was really scared. I had lost my leader! That was any wingman's principal nightmare. What in hell had happened? I hadn't heard a word out of Carter when he dove out of formation. Where had he gone? Did he get back O.K.? Godamnit!

Percy let me out of the jeep at the line shack where we stored our chutes and gear and where we were debriefed by Intelligence after a mission. I slung my chute and Mae West over my shoulder and trudged up the walk to the entrance. Major Bochkay came out to meet me.

"What happened, pal?" he said, with a poker face that disclosed nothing.

I gulped a couple of times and started at the beginning of that day's events. I told him as concisely as I could what had transpired. When I finished, he stuck out his paw, and his concrete jaw relaxed into a lopsided grin.

"You're O.K., sport," he said. "Carter's radio malfunctioned. We checked it out. No one else, including me, heard him announce he was leaving the formation. I can't say I was really surprised when you took out after him. Good show, Matey," he said in a phony cockney dialect.

Suddenly I wasn't tired anymore. At the same time I wasn't proud of what had happened. If I had been looking at Carter when he peeled off, it would have been so simple. I'd have gone with him. I never discussed the matter with Carter. I don't know what he told them at his debriefing, but he never offered me any explanation and I didn't ask.

So you see, Donald, me boy. I am not the Stone Age guy I thought I might be. I'm not sure of the difference between scared, apprehensive, fearful, etc. But I sure as hell prefer actual combat to solo operations deep inside Germany.

I'm due for a 48-hour pass tomorrow. I may get sloshed tonight.

Alan

"My God! Pardon me, Chaplain, but it would be a hundred times worse than Saturday night with no mission on Sunday. Hell...pardon me 'Chappie,' but you'd have a hundred Limey broads coming out of the woodwork. There'd be...heck to pay." Captain Earhardt, chief of security of the Leiston Airdrome, had difficulty conversing with the committee that included Chaplain Lewis.

The 363rd Fighter Squadron was first formed at Hamilton Field, California on the 8th of December, 1942. This year, 1944, the 8th of December fell on a Friday, just three weeks away. The squadron was determined to have an anniversary celebration.

Captain Monroe, group meteorologist, was immediately the most important source of intelligence to the plans being considered for this "war game." He had everyone's attention.

"Group Captain J. N. Stagg of the Royal Air Force, as you may recall, was the chief meteorologist of Overland, who, with his associates advised General Eisenhower on the anticipated weather conditions for May 6, D-Day. I wish he was here to help forecast this operation."

Captain Monroe was dead serious. He was well aware of the difficulties it would present, if the 357th was assigned a mission on December 9, Saturday, the day after the planned blow-out.

A dozen anxious cries interrupted Captain Monroe's scholarly dissertation; "Get on with it 'Soupy'; what's the goddamn weather going to be?; To hell with D-Day, that's history. What's it look like for the ninth?"

Captain "Soupy" Monroe raised his hands and said quietly, "I wish I could tell you for sure."

"Alright," said Squadron Commander Bochkay, "what are the odds? We know you can't guarantee it."

Monroe stood looking at the sheaf of papers in his hand. He was putting his technical mind to work in the manner of a race track tout. Odds, was it? He finally spoke.

"I'd say...that the odds are 4 to 1, that it will storm like hell on Saturday, December 9th. It should be a dawn-day."

The room erupted with cheers and whistles.

"That'a a helluva lot better odds than we have of surviving this goddamn war," said Major "Bock." "Let's do it!"

The anniversary party plan was a simple one. Booze and broads. Group Headquarters Master Sergeant Mahoney, who knew everything and everyone on the base and off it, was unanimously elected as chairman of the event. As usual, he performed. A band was retained from a nearby Ipswich club, and a group of Leiston village belles, supported by the group's nurses, were enlisted to take care of the decorations. Mahoney called a meeting of the mess sergeants of all three squadrons, and they readily "volunteered" to prepare plenty of "horse's ovaries" (hors d'oeuvres), and enough pastries to feed an army, or in this case, a group.

The logistics of the operation were well in hand. All that remained were the invitations.

"How in hell am I going to get a date?" Lieutenant Aaron asked the others gathered at the officers' club bar. "All the gals I've met in London only have first names. And I've never met the same one twice."

Many of those in earshot had the same problem. None of the pilots visited the local pubs with any regularity. If they were flying the next day, they didn't carouse the night before. Having a clear head in the morning, rather than a hangover, was the cheapest life insurance they could buy. The available local ladies that lived near the house were well wooed by the enlisted men. The fighter jocks waited for their periodic 48-hour passes, and headed for Piccadilly Circus in London, where they found plenty of targets of opportunity.

"Well, most of us will get a 48 before then, and that's when we'll have to line up a date," said Enfield. "Sarge said he'd arrange transportation to the base from the train station at Leiston, and also for the local girls who are invited."

"That's just great, if you've got someone coming on the train," said Aaron. "I'm sure as hell not looking forward to dancing with Sarge."

It had been planned originally to just use the officers' club and mess hall for the affair that was to entertain all base personnel. It soon became apparent that the facilities of the noncom club and the enlisted personnel mess hall would also be required to accommodate the throng that was now expected. Another band, another decorating committee was recruited by Master Sergeant Mahoney, and the mess sergeants added "can-of-peas" (canapes) to their party menus.

It was going to be a real "bash." The names of "dates" that had been arranged appeared on Captain Earhardt's A Security List that got longer and longer. Many memos were issued spelling out in great detail how the safety and comfort of the guests was to be assured.

The one item that somehow was overlooked in all of the planning was expressed belatedly by Chappie Lewis, who asked on the eve of the party, "Where will all of the ladies sleep?"

Dear Lolly,

Can you believe it? It's been three years since Pearl Harbor. And, there's only 17 more shopping days until Xmas. Well, that's one deadline I won't have to worry about. I hope my present has gotten to you by now. I worry about its being breakable, but Percy, my crew chief packed it for me and he doesn't do anything halfway. I'll bet it made it O.K. I got your package, and one of the things looks and feels like a loaf of bread, except it gurgles when I shake it. You don't suppose!

It's kind of hard to get in a holiday spirit. We've got Christmas trees all over the place like the Officer's Club, the N.C.O. Club, the PX, the mess halls and even in the Quonset quarters. It's real nice, but in a way I almost wish we'd forget it until we get home and do it right. If I hear "Silent Night", or "Deck the Halls" one more time on the P.A. system I think I'll go nuts. C'est la Yule!

I hope I don't bore you or depress you with a couple of things that have really been bugging me more or less lately.

First, I've been feeling a little guilty about my religious beliefs. I know that over-used saying by Bill Mauldin or Ernie Pyle or someone, about there are "no atheists in fox holes." But I got to tell you I don't personally know one of the guys I fly with that goes to mass or church, or says his prayers kneeling by the side of his bunk. I don't know what they do privately, but they sure don't make a big thing out of religion in the open. You know that I was baptized in the Episcopal Church there at home, and Mom saw to it that I went to Sunday School every Sunday 'till I got old enough to worm my way out of it. But the main thing I remember was the "Reverend" Mr. Snyder (that tub of lard) and his isolationist sermons that used to make Dad so mad. And the "professional weepers" that used to turn up at every funeral whether they knew the departed or not. Boy, I don't know. That all seems pretty silly in a place like this. Oh, I believe in a God alright. But I don't beg of Him, or promise a whole lot. But, sometimes at 20,000 feet when we're finally on our way home, and we're flying over a pure white overcast towards the late afternoon sun, it's hard not to believe some super being created all that. I just wish he cared a little more about letting people start wars, and killing a lot of really great guys.

Well, enough of that stuff. I probably won't bore you again with my "Philosophy," but you're the only one I can talk to like this. It isn't the great bar conversation.

We're having a big party tomorrow night. The 357 Fighter Group was formed two years ago, December 8, and with the weather socked in, we're going to "tie one on." Looks like this is a major storm that will last for three or four days, so we've got some time off. I'm really glad for that. It's been a little rough lately, and my crew can stand a rest. I know I can.

We're seeing huge numbers of enemy aircraft on occasion these days. They say (whoever that is) that Goering is sending up cadets and everyone that can fly at all in a desperate final effort. I hope that's right. Their flak is still pretty good, and weather this time of year is by far the biggest hazard. Not that those clouds with rocks in 'em are any fun. But, we've got the bit in our teeth and we're going to win this one. Bet on it.

You're the last person I think about every night. I know someday we're going to be together again.

You can be sure I believe in that.

> All my love,
> Alan

The 357th did not fly a mission on December 8. The 8th Air Force did not fly a mission on December 8. No mission would be flown on December 9. Captain James Monroe, it was unanimously agreed, should be promoted to General Monroe. His weather was beautiful. The worst storm of the year blew in, full force, out of the Northeast, and stopped all action in the air, and a lot of activity on the ground, except for the trains from London, and the shuttle vehicles from the nearby towns of Saxemundam and Leiston. And, the storm was to continue raging for at least two days.

No amount of rain, wind and sleet could dampen the spirits of this party. The ladies arrived throughout the stormy afternoon and early evening, and were escorted to the Visiting V.I.P. quarters which had been vacated for them. There, they got out of their travelling garb and rain gear, and changed into their party clothes. The transformation was magic. Everyone was beautiful, their escorts were absolutely delighted, and the old Leiston Airdrome had never had it so good.

The sounding of the air raid siren at 2:00 A.M. signalled the end of the scheduled festivities in both clubs. The bands, to loud applause, had played last tunes at midnight. Action in the pilots' lounge hardly missed a beat. "Chappie" Lewis had a hidden talent he'd never disclosed. He played the damndest jazz piano anyone had ever heard anywhere. "Chappie" took up where the bands left off. And the good times rolled!

Casualties of the night were few. Oh, there were a couple of minor incidents. A certain lieutenant got minor cuts when he met with an "enemy barbed wire entanglement," as he described a three-strand fence he tried to navigate while walking his "local date" home in the wee hours just before dawn. A J.B., junior birdman, newly assigned to B Flight, was ordered on a "Mission of Mercy." He was dispatched to proceed to the officers' mess and acquire, by threat or bribe, a resupply of liquid and solid provisions desperately required at B Flight's Quonset hut where an after hours soiree was taking place. The J.B. proved worthy of the task, and on his bicycle handle bars, he carefully balanced a huge tray loaded with his loot, and started back through the still raging storm. He nearly made it. He crashed not 50 feet from the Quonset he was homed in on. It was literally a nose-dive. Hitting a hidden ditch, he went headfirst over the handle bars, and landed smack in the middle of the tray. When rescued, he was wearing most of the pastries and other foodstuffs he'd requisitioned.

But not one bottle was even cracked! He was awarded, with proper ceremony, the "W.C. With Chain."

The chief of security had most of the problems he had anticipated at the very beginning, in enforcing the various regulations that could apply to civilians visiting his base. Captain Earhardt had briefed his staff thoroughly, and issued numerous memos concerning every eventuality he could visualize. Most of the incidents he anticipated did occur, but few, in fact none, of the regulations that were "bent" were enforced. The M.P.s on duty that night, "due to the storm, the noise of the gale, and the limited visibility," found it impossible to distinguish between enlisted and officer personnel. Indeed, it was equally impossible to identify a "guest" shrouded in a huge parka, or, on at least one occasion, wrapped in an army blanket.

"Chappie" Lewis, who had expressed earlier concern as to sleeping accommodations for the visitors, needn't have worried. Any that accepted the hospitality of their hosts for the night's lodging were even provided with room service.

There was no ribbon attached to the "W.C. with Chain" award, so it was not displayed with the array of "fruit salad" that appeared on the blouses of combat veterans. It was a sort of British decoration. It was not thought of as an award for heroism, though there were some that would disagree. Its origins are unknown. The symbolism is vague.

Most hostelries and some homes throughout England, if they had plumbing, had a toilet, or loo as they called it. The main device in this sanitary facility was of a unique design, at least to Americans. The seat portion was the same. But, the source of water that supplied the convenience, came from a tank, often made of hardwood lined with zinc, that was mounted some five or six feet above, on the wall behind the seat. This provided a reliable source of pressure and flow due to gravity. In order to trigger this water closet (W.C.), you pulled on a chain that hung conveniently at hand. It worked beautifully. The noise was deafening. The W.C. with Chain, somehow, was associated in the minds of the Yanks with London.

An award ceremony for bestowing this honor was sometimes staged at the "Pussycat," a private membership-only club in Piccadilly that many of the pilots in the 8th Air Force belonged to. There, it was legal to drink after curfew, when the pubs and bars had to close, if you were a member. The charge for becoming a member was about $1.00 American.

A new "pledge," upon receiving his first 48-hour pass after going "operational," was ordered to report to the "Pussycat" upon his arrival in Piccadilly. There he was met by the "Initiation Committee," and was welcomed, and plied with generous libations. When the evening advanced, and the pledge was properly relaxed, he was introduced to his "date" for the night. Qualifications to be a "date" did not require pulchritude, youth, or intellect. She need only be willing. She was usually recruited from the many Nightingales of the Night who greeted their possible customers on the London streets with, "'Ave a go chum, yer Mum won't know." They were rarely ex-beauty queens.

The following evening, depending on the account given by the pledge of his experiences during the preceding night, he was awarded the "W.C. with Chain," and he was now permitted to buy the drinks. For the remainder of his time left on leave, he was required to wear his W.C. with Chain draped over his left shoulder like a French fleur-de-lis. Throughout "the Circus" he was a marked man for the remainder of that stay.

The best account about the infantry war on the ground in this war was undoubtedly those weekly reports filed by Ernie Pyle back to the folks at home. These graphic articles and the cartoons submitted by Bill Mauldin showed dramatically what a dirty business ground war was. I and most of my mates in the flying business talked about this "other war," and no one among the combat flyers would have changed places with their comrades in the mud.

There were few things ground and air personnel had in common. It's true, they both had learned to kill impersonally, and in many cases, without hate. They both faced an enemy that had to be destroyed whether in a Messerschmidt or a machine gun nest. There was little distinction between an aircraft or a tank and the human beings that occupied these weapons of destruction. There's no doubt there was a feeling of relief, even victorious satisfaction when the enemy that was trying to kill you was eliminated.

But when the conflict of the day was over, the sky-fighters went home to a secure haven, a change to fresh clothes, a few drinks at the club, a hot dinner in the officers' mess, a few hands of bridge or poker, a movie and on to bed between sheets.

Compare this combat duty to those waging Pyle's "Ernie's War," or the tedious efforts of Mauldin's bedraggled Willie and Joe, the GI Grunts depicted in his grim cartoons. When these warriors had to kill it was many times face to face with the enemy. And when it was finally over for that day, it was K rations, a search for someplace to sleep other than a muddy foxhole, or finally a place where you just flopped down on the sodden earth in utter exhaustion. That's the "dirty war," and "UP FRONT" was a far cry from "UP THERE."

There was possibly one balancing factor. Reported casualties in a fighter group rarely reflected any injuries. When a pilot "bought it" in combat, he either burned in flames, perished in the crash, or was executed in his chute. There were no medics at 20,000 feet.

The only time fighter pilots came even close to the "dirty war" was when they provided ground support, strafing missions against troops and equipment on the ground. For the 357th pilots such tactical assignments were usually tacked onto high altitude bomber escort missions after they had herded the heavies back to safe territory and then hit the deck to strike "targets of opportunity."

These "targets," usually identified in a split second at 300 mph, varied from ground troops, trucks, tanks, artillery emplacements, and regrettably, on one occasion, a wedding party of German soldiers coming out of a church.

Trains, specifically locomotives, were the most fun. Fun is a strange word to use, but there's none other that describes the exhilaration that comes with seeing a towering explosion of hot metal and steam billowing up in the sky. The action was not without hazard. If the attacking aircraft closed too tight on its target it would be unable to fly through the cloud of iron fragments without being destroyed. Additionally, the ingenious Germans had created camouflaged box cars whose roofs and sides would collapse when attacked to disclose heavily armed flak platforms that would throw up a curtain of tracers and shrapnel. If you survived the initial pass, you didn't dare return for another run. Some overly eager, relatively green jockeys tried it, and the results were fatal.

Strafing airdromes, destroying aircraft on the ground, was equally satisfying and related directly to the elimination of an enemy competitor whom you might be facing in combat the next day in the sky. These missions were usually one-passing-attack affairs, and relied heavily on the element of surprise. The target was approached at tree top level, and line-abreast, 8 or 12 fighters would rake the aircraft hard-stands and revetments alongside the enemy runways with their 50 calibres, and be succeeded by subsequent waves of attacking fighters, the number of which would depend upon whether it was a squadron or a group effort. These raids destroyed enemy aircraft not manned with pilots, but they too were fun.

Some groups in the 8th Air Force late in the war credited their pilots with "victories" for aircraft destroyed on the ground. The 357th Fighter Group did not adopt this policy, and there wasn't an Ace among the Yoxford Boys that included any ground kills in his record of enemy planes "destroyed, damaged or probables" combat record.

I came as close to being shot down on one of these "fun missions" as I had in many engagements in the air.

"I was the last plane on the left flank of the second wave." I was relating that day's events to Sergeant Blount, my crew chief, who was unusually interested in the strafing mission just completed.

"There weren't any parked planes on my side close to the edge of the narrow field. Ground fire was pretty intense and I was kicking rudders and shooting any vehicles, gun emplacements, shacks and a water tower when I finally ran out aerodrome and targets and made a vertical turn to the left, lifted slightly to clear some trees at the edge of the field, and just then, I heard a metallic clang like a gong being struck."

"That's weird, Cap," Blount said. "What did you think it was?"

"I didn't have time to figure it out just then," I continued. "About the same time I was suddenly confronted with a huge windmill in my path that I barely avoided by swerving through a Vee formed by its unmoving vanes. I missed the mill, but I clipped the top off a haystack beyond the mill as I got away from the following ground fire. I was a little worried about damage from projectiles, or the hay I might have packed into my belly scoop, but *Daisy Mae* flew great, and no coolant or oil temperature problems occurred."

Sergeant Blount listened to this account with great interest. Now, he looked down at an object he held in his hand. He had first seen it when I rolled back my canopy while Blount was standing on the wing ready to help me unbuckle and dismount. There, imbedded in the back of the vehicle armor plate behind the pilot's seat, near the top of the shield where the pilot's head rest is located on the opposite side, was a 20 mm projectile.

"I guess that explains the gong you heard, Cap," Blount said seriously. "I knew you were a damn good pilot, but I didn't know you were also the luckiest jock in the E.T.O."

I was rather relieved to learn during bull sessions with other combat pilots that they too had done some rather stupid things while flying locally when no combat mission was scheduled. It was common practice for many pilots to try to fly every day in order to maintain the fine edge of proficiency that's essential in winning a crucial contest with a formidable enemy. It was amazing how rusty one would feel after a short 48-hour pass to London that provided a brief rest and certainly a change of pace from the usual routine. The "Battle of Piccadilly Circus" was great fun, and provided a different kind of fatigue that was a welcome relief. But these brief intervals did interrupt the rhythm of daily combat flying, and it did require a brief adjustment to regain top flying performance.

My one experience that demonstrated the hazards of "casual flying" came on a visit I arranged to spend a pass I had coming with my oldest brother Burr whom I hadn't seen in nearly three years. He was serving as a bombsight specialist sergeant stationed at Norwich AFB located some 40 or 50 miles northerly from our base at Leiston. I had a fabulous reunion with Burr and greatly enjoyed two nights in his N.C.O. quarters playing cards and sipping some Johnny Walker Red.

The next day Burr arranged my getting a right seat co-pilot's slot on a local B-17 bomber flight that really opened my eyes as to the abilities of these great Big Boy jocks.

On the last morning in Norwich with just a couple of hours left on my 48-hour pass, I had a final early breakfast with Burr and most of his Quonset mates and then hurried to the flight line where *Daisy Mae*, my Mustang, awaited my return hop back to R85, Leiston.

As I taxied past the ramp in front of the control tower, I noticed that Burr and a bunch of his pals were there in force waving and giving me a thumbs up to speed me on my way.

Ah ha! I thought. I must give them a little gesture of my appreciation for their hospitality.

I made a high speed take off run getting airborne just a couple of feet off the runway, sucked up my wheels and at about 130 mph indicated roared on the deck towards the north end of the field that was bordered by some leafy trees and bushes about 25 or 30 feet in height. I clipped the tops of this foliage, raised the nose slightly and started a victory slow roll. It was a lousy slow roll! I "dished out" at the top of the roll and my slow roll became a barrel roll, the bottom of which is unknown due to the inevitable loss of altitude.

There is no doubt I would have crashed except for the fact that the terrain beyond the perimeter of the aerodrome sloped down and away some 50 or more feet, giving me some air to regain level flight and then a climbing altitude.

"How stupid can you get? Boy, you're shot in the ass with luck today, sport"; and other not so polite criticisms that I swore aloud to an audience of one.

I managed a careful and conservative pattern and landing back at my home base, taxied in, and after cutting my engine and alighting to the tarmac at my hardstand, I was approached by my C.O., Major Bochkay, who had obviously been waiting for me in his jeep.

"I've got a message for you, Ab," he said, and he wasn't wearing his usual grin. "I got a call from a Sergeant Abner at Norwich, and he was a little steamed. He respectfully requested that you call him immediately upon arrival. He didn't say what he was concerned about, but take care of it pronto!"

I did place the call as ordered, and got a chewing out from Sergeant Abner that equalled the most vehement, most descriptive invective I'd heard since my worst days in Primary Flying School. And he was right. Showin' off ain't habit formin'.

Alan Abner with brother, Burr, at Norwich Air Force Base in 1944.

***Daisy Mae*, European Theatre of Operations in 1945.**

CHAPTER VII *BATTLE OF THE BULGE*

The 357th's weather expert, Captain "Soupy" Monroe, had accurately predicted the storm that allowed the anniversary party to take place uninterrupted by any mission activity. The months of December and November had been a period of increasing downtimes as the winter storms became more frequent. The 8th Air Force was occupied during this period with their customary strategic role of escorting the heavies to targets in Germany that produced aircraft, materials of war, fuel and destroying lines of travel and communication.

But the weather was on the side of the enemy. The November rains had been the worst in many years, and though the allied ground forces had driven the Wehrmacht back to within 50 to 100 miles of the Rhine along a 250-mile front, the lowlands along rivers and streams made a quagmire through which the infantry and mobile units had to struggle.

The Ardennes, in keeping with its World War I history, became the scene of this war's greatest crisis since D-Day.

Eisenhower's decision to strike hard from Aachen in the north as well as through Alsace in the south had left the center relatively weak. Though the fighting lessened somewhat in early December, bad flying weather hindered allied efforts to accurately assess what the enemy was doing. What they were doing was preparing a last desperate assault that was to become the Battle of the Bulge.

Hitler, with the advice of his astrologer and the tacit approval of his general staff, gave Von Rundstadt the green light, and the

101

brilliant German general quietly assembled two Panzer armies, the Fifth and Sixth, the Seventh Army, making a total of ten Panzer divisions, and fourteen Infantry Divisions. Led by its armor, the intention was to break through the Ardennes to the river Meuse, turn north and northwest, cut the allied line in two, seize the Port of Antwerp, and sever the lifeline of the Allied Northern Armies. All available resources in addition to the conventional were mustered. What was left of the Luftwaffe was assembled and readied. Paratroops were poised, as well as saboteurs and agents in allied uniforms, and captured enemy planes were assigned their roles.

The German surprise attack began on December 16 and continued in full force until December 26. At one time the German forces were only 4 miles from the Meuse, and had penetrated over 60 miles. Bad weather and ground fog had handicapped allied air forces for the first week, but on December 23, flying conditions improved and air power joined the battles with tremendous effect. The Heavies attacked rail centers behind the lines and the Ninth Air Force Thunderbolts stormed into the fray on the ground. The bomber crews unleashed raids on oil depots and refineries that denied ground vehicles fuel and stalled the German efforts.

Despite their defeat the Germans continued to give battle west of the Rhine throughout January and February instead of withdrawing across the historic river to more defensible positions.

For the pilots of the 357th Fighter Group the nature of their participation in the war changed dramatically.

As the war raged on the ground and despite the weather, scheduling missions for the Eighth Air Force and the fighter groups were dependent more on the cloud cover over targets than on ceiling and visibility minimums at home. It was not uncommon for our group to take off with a 300-foot ceiling, climb through a 16,000-foot solid overcast to pick up the bombers on their way to their target "ON TOP." More fighter pilots were lost due to weather than were casualties of combat during this period.

Another element was now added to this already hazardous format. Now, after escorting the bombers to the target, and when the Big Boys were reasonably safe for their return trip back to the U.K., the fighters would find a "hole" in the overcast, dive through to ground level and attack any "Targets of Opportunity" they could find on their low-level sweep back to terrain occupied by friendly forces.

Targets of opportunity included anything military on the ground: airdromes, motor pools, convoys, troops, ammunition dumps, fuel depots, artillery, barges and perhaps best of all, railroad equipment.

"I was almost too close when that locomotive blew." I was describing my day's events to the intelligence debriefer. "Boy. When they go up, that cloud of steam and smoke is plumb full of iron. And you know, the hard way, that it's almost fatal to fly through it. That's how Riley and Borden both bought it early on. I didn't notice whether there were any flak cars in the line. I was pretty busy."

Down-time bull sessions now had a new topic that dominated the subject matter under discussion. A statement that would have been considered blasphemous a few weeks earlier now was expressed more and more frequently.

"In air-to-air combat I wouldn't trade the Mustang for any plane on earth. But, damnit, they aren't made for ground support missions."

It was true. It *was* the best high performance fighter in the skies... "but at low level it can be knocked down with a bee-bee gun!"

The P-51's Rolls Royce Merlin engine was liquid cooled. And the yards of coolant tubing that supplied the engine with its precious fluid could be easily penetrated. When that happened, the engine would freeze in a matter of minutes and it would be "hit the silk."

"I got a letter the other day from an old buddy of mine from back home that's flying T Bolts with the 9th." I had corresponded with Dave Boss who had joined up when I did. "Dave said his bird was almost indestructible. He'd made it home more than once with one or two cylinders shot out on that big, radial air cooled engine. He's been flying ground-support, mostly for Patton's third Army, and he wouldn't trade us one T-Bolt for ten Mustangs for the job they've got to do."

Strafing locomotives was "fun," but his new assignment did fill our mission requirements that were already rather heavy.

Sorties now were not uncommon that required 4 to 6 hours in the air for completion. The climb after takeoff took 35 to 45 minutes of instrument formation flying. Another couple of hours or so of high altitude escort of the bombers to the ever deepening target areas, and return after the bombing run to a point where the heavies were reasonably secure from enemy aerial attack. And, of course, occasional dog fights when the Luftwaffe decided to come up for the day. Then on the deck, under the overcast, often in rain and fog, in a ground support combat role. And sometimes, the worst was yet to come.

Homeward bound at last, crossing the Channel at an altitude oftentimes less than 200 feet, in the teeth of a gale out of the

North Sea with freezing rain, and winds churning the steel-gray waters with white caps, and you hoped your gas gauges were correct. You also hoped you'd recognize a landmark on the English coast that would identify your position, north or south of the home base. Assuming you did find the old wooden derrick on the beach that marked the end of the Leiston runway 3 miles inland, and you were finally cleared to land...then you modified the typical tactical fighter approach to landing by leaning the usual vertical loop, overhead 360-degree pattern so you didn't climb up into the threatening overcast. Another routine day.

The German offensive into the Ardennes was broken, but the Wehrmacht continued to give battle west of the Rhine through February and into March. Their slowly retreating defense was strong, the earth was a quagmire, and both the Rhine and the Meuse overflowed their banks. The Nazi sappers smashed the valves on the huge dams on the Roer River and it was impassable until the end of February. By March 10, eighteen of the twenty-four German divisions were back across the Rhine, but the stubborn remaining rear guard gave ground grudgingly, and sectors were frequently lost and retaken during these last days of the Bulge counteroffensive.

The fighter jocks of the 357th and the other 8th A.F. fighter groups had become accustomed to their additional role, waging ground attacks on Targets of Opportunity. It really was pretty exciting duty. Treetop-level flying, clobbering anything that appeared as a target on the way back to the Channel and home. One high speed pass at the target, and on to the next opportunity.

It was very distracting to the enemy, and it was as much fun as war can be fun, but it was not ground support as practiced by the 9th Air Force Tactical groups. The Republic Thunderbolt P-47s functioned more as a highly mobile artillery arm, and attacked specific targets designated by the area command. This wasn't hit-and-run strafing. This was the methodical destruction of the enemy forces on the ground, and if it took ten passes to do the job, they did it. And the T-Bolts they were flying were the best aircraft in the world for the job at hand.

"Yesterday, the First U.S. Army's 9th Armored Division captured the railway bridge at Remagen. The Krauts are methodically trying to blow up all of the bridges across the Rhine in order to slow down our attacks on their retreating forces." Major Stevens, Intelligence briefing officer, though always calm and usually phlegmatic, seemed more intense than usual this morning. "The Ninth Air Force guys are doing their jobs in great fashion as usual, but our orders from Wing have instructed us to help them out a little. I'm sure you all recognize the importance of saving the remaining bridges from destruction for the use of our advancing forces. It's vital to the maintenance of our momentum and our ultimate success in crushing the German armies who are still fighting, but on the run. Taking Remagen was the good news. Today's mission is ground support strafing on targets along the eastern side of the Rhine River."

"I never did like over-water flying," said Captain Carter after the briefing as he and his flight members crawled into a jeep that would take them to the flight line. "I'll bet the water in that Rhine River is cold as ice. In fact, it is probably mostly ice."

Lieutenant Fifield, driving the vehicle as if he were already on a strafing run, agreed.

"Yeah. That river is pretty wide in spots, and fairly deep I'm told. But I suspect the problem is going to be by land rather than by sea."

I nodded seriously. "No doubt. I don't want to sound disloyal to *Daisy Mae*, but today I think I'd rather be flying one of Dave Boss's T Bolts than my Mustang. She just isn't used to such harsh treatment."

The weather, for a change, was halfway decent over England, and the 4,000-foot overcast was forecasted to extend across western Europe to the target areas. Fighter groups from all over the United Kingdom swept across the battle-torn Continent like an armada of landing craft attacking the beaches. Our flight had drawn the right flank, end position, of the 363rd Squadron. Major Bochkay signaled them into a long north to south line-abreast formation some 20 miles west of the Rhine River to the east. It was the last formal formation of the day.

Each pilot was more or less on his own. He'd seek his own targets, attack until his ammunition was gone, and return to designated area and regroup if possible. Wingmen were not required to protect their leader from attacks from enemy aircraft because none were expected, and none appeared.

My sector included two bridges across the river at Duesseldorf, one at the south end of the city which appeared to have been destroyed, and another north, near the city center whose central span seemed to be intact. I had strafed a motor convoy while approaching the city down an Autobahn from the west, and swung left of the damaged bridge up the river to fire at some barges and small craft that appeared to carry work forces headed for the remaining span. A gun emplacement near the end of the bridge on its east bank opened up on my Mustang, but a kick of the rudders and the six 50 calibres in *Daisy Mae* quickly silenced them. I made my final run some 20 minutes later a few miles north of the city on an airfield later designated as Lohausen, strafing down a line of parked JU-88s in their revetments, and turned toward the west and the river when my gun loads ran out. It was here that the ground fire was most intense, and it was with relief that I found my bird could still fly, and the job was done.

"Boy! Torry Torrance was sure right back at Aloe. This sure as hell ain't habit forming." As was my habit, I talked to myself when coming out of a tight situation. And that last run certainly qualified as a tight situation.

Streaking at a very low level across the Rhine away from the ground fire and heading towards the "friendlies," my Mustang coughed a couple of times, belched some black smoke, and the big prop began to lose rotation.

"What the hell," I yelled, when I had just begun to relax a little. Out of gas? Quickly I reached down to the fuel selector on the floor in front of the stick, and switched from the right wing tank where it was positioned, to the left tank that I'd drawn on earlier. A heart-stopping split second and the engine caught as the new fuel source fed in and power was resumed. But this was a new, serious problem.

Climbing to an altitude now of about 1,000 feet, I took inventory. The right tank was obviously dry, and I had run earlier on the left wing tank until we had formed up for our attack on the target area. The fuselage tank had been used first for take-off and climb-out and its 85-gallon capacity had been reduced to 25 or so gallons to establish a stable center of gravity to the aircraft for best maneuverability for the low level chores ahead. Looking over my left shoulder I read the fuselage tank gauge and confirmed. The left wing tank obviously still had some fuel remaining, but I knew it wasn't enough to get home...I knew I had to find a place to sit down, and be sure it was on a friendly field.

Continuing westward at reduced power, I anxiously scanned the tattered, war torn terrain for a field that could accommodate a high speed fighter aircraft. The surface below bore little resemblance to those Texas tracts where I'd practiced endless forced landings in the old Fairchild trainer bi-plane, but the problem was the same.

Suddenly, at a 45 degree angle off my nose to the left, was a fairly large open space with a grass field that even displayed a wind sock! A number of big trucks, jeeps and weapons carriers bearing American markings were scattered on the east side of the clearing. Turning in a shallow bank I circled the field, waggling my wings. I could detect a strip of matted grass that obviously had been used as the landing and takeoff area. The strip was situated in a north-south configuration, and the wind sock was pointed almost directly to the north, so that was something at least.

Turning southward at the northwest corner of the field I cut throttle even with the spot where I wanted to touch down, put down full flaps and started my base leg turn. Wheels down, I turned on final approach, full flaps, and with a couple of fish tails, dropped the bird to about five feet off the ground, stalled, and pancaked, 3 points on the soft, spongy surface. I was down.

Cutting the engine and rolling back the canopy, I looked out to see a master sergeant as big as a house getting out of jeep that had pulled up alongside.

Climbing up onto the wing, the sarge grinned at me, as I was wiping the sweat off my forehead, and said, "You looked like you might have done that trick a few times before, sir."

"No, Sarge," I responded, "that's the first time, and I hope to Christ it's the last."

Master Sergeant McAllister was in command of a platoon of army engineers who had lost their lieutenant C.O. in a skirmish two days before. It seemed this was the second time they had occupied this field located a few miles east of Muenchen Gladbach, having been routed a couple of days earlier as the volatile ground engagements swung back and forth, and they had only relocated the previous night. The sarge, like many of his breed, was a man who took charge and got things done.

When told of the events that led to the forced landing, Mac, as he insisted I call him, put a couple of his best mechanics to the task of determining the damage to the gas lines, and began searching for solutions to the problem.

We, a mechanic and Sarge, stood leaning against the side of the big 8 by 8 equipment truck that had pulled up and parked alongside of the aircraft. The mechanics had found the holes under the right wing where the 30 mms had entered the fuselage. They had removed the damaged panels and were probing the interior, looking for the rupture.

"Let's see," Sarge said, staring at me. "You've got three tanks, two in the wings and the one behind the seat. I had them put a stick to 'em, and the right tank is empty, the left's got about 20 gallons in it, and the seat tank has about 24. And I know without askin' that it must be 100 octane fuel at least."

The crew found the break in the line to the right wing tank and Mac decided to block it from the rest of the fuel system rather than attempt to repair it. With that done, and with some misgivings, they diluted the remaining aviation gas in the left wing tank with 60 gallons of 86 octane fuel they had on hand after straining it through a half dozen layers of cloth. They left the fuselage tank with its fuel intact to be used for take-off and later, if there was any left, for landing.

"I think a running engine, as fine a machine as that 12 cylinder Rolls Royce will handle it," Sarge said. "You got the good gas for take-off, and I think you'll be O.K. Oh, I had the strip measured... 2,300 feet to the end, and another 150 feet to that power line across the end of the field. It's only on 20-foot poles so I wouldn't recommend you go under it."

I looked at the big man with genuine admiration and some amusement. "I'm sure sorry I only have one seat in that bird or you could come along for the ride. Seems like that's the least I could do for you after all you guys have done for me."

"Well, that's O.K.", Sarge replied with a grin. "Maybe some other time. Maybe we'll have a drink on it once this damn fracas is over."

The engineers lifted the tail of the Mustang, tied the wheel to the back of a jeep and towed me and my bird to the south end of the strip where the vertical rudder was almost hidden by the higher grass. A stout rope was looped onto the tail wheel, carefully slip-knotted, with the other end snubbed to a tree. The "launch" was in readiness.

Starting the engine, I only waited at 1000 RPMs until the gauges started up toward the "green," lowered 15 degrees of flaps and poured on full power. The Mustang trembled and strained forward, the rope was released and the "half wild horse of Texas," as the Brits had named her, roared down the fairway.

The dips and bumps in the surface of the run had probably not been noticed by the reconnaissance aircraft that had used it. But the fighter bounced from one rise to the next like a crow-hopping Cayuse. Finally, less than a 150 yards or so from the fence, it lifted. I sucked up the wheels and cleared the inevitable power line by at least 10 feet.

A shallow climbing turn to the left, a waggle of wings to my comrades on the ground, and I headed west.

"Roger Cement 79, this is Earlduke." Tilly Botti. That laconic voice that never changed, responded immediately upon my radio request. "You are cleared for a straight in approach on runway 24. Do you require any emergency equipment?"

"Negative Earlduke," I replied. "Just low on juice and wouldn't care to go around."

"Rog, Cement 79. Happy landing," Earlduke concluded.

When I landed, Crew Chief Blount was waiting on the taxiway at the far end of the runway and jumped up to ride in on the wing as I slowly made the turn. The turn was rather jumpy as the tail wheel refused to swivel, probably as a result of being hog-tied before that last take-off. It proved to be the only structural damage to the aircraft.

Taylor, Crawford, Myers and "J.B." Andrus were waiting in a jeep at the hardstand as B6-R slowly parked.

"What'd you do? Stop in Berlin for a beer?" Taylor stated flatly as I clamored aboard the jeep, sitting on the hood.

"Yeah," said their "intrepid" comrade. "Ground support makes me real thirsty. Let's go."

There is one facility the government planners, the people that designed military installations for combat airmen didn't provide. A place to be alone. A combat infantryman would find considerable amusement in this problem, and would probably recommend a fox hole if someone "wanted to be alone"! But it was true.

Of course there's a cubicle in the latrine if you can avoid the rush hour. Then there's the base chapel. But suppose you weren't particularly interested in divine guidance. Your bunk in the Quonset where you're quartered with a dozen other pilots can be sort of a sanctuary if you pretend to be asleep. But you're sure to be rousted for a fourth at bridge, or a trip to the club for a game of snooker. Sitting alone in a dark corner of the pilots' lounge, brooding over a beer could start all sorts of speculations. Such as: "I wonder if old Ab' got a Dear John?...Maybe he's got the clap...How many missions does Cap have to go?...That broad in Ipswitch surely isn't...No!" and so on.

I finally found a secret place, and so far, no one had discovered it. On rare occasions I'd grab my bike, rain or sleet, and peddle it to the flight line, lie to the sentries and sit in my airplane.

It was kind of like a businessman turning off the lights and sitting in his skyscraper office looking down at his city after hours. After all, the cockpit was my place of business, and there wasn't any room for outside intrusion or distracting conversation.

For the first time I really felt intimidated. Goddamn! That really was pretty hairy. Suppose that power line had been 10 feet taller. Suppose I'd run out of gas over the Channel? Percy said I did have enough or more to go around if I'd screwed up the landing, but I sure as hell didn't know that at the time. It's just like I told Don. I don't remember ever being scared. Maybe I don't know what being scared is. It's like I told him, you're so goddamn busy solving problems you don't have time to be scared.

Well, right now I have time. And I think I was a little scared. I'm not afraid that I won't be able to perform. The training I got took care of that. I'll perform all right even if I'm scared shitless. But so far I haven't been. And I'm damned if that's going to change. I know Grandad would agree.

But today was different. Maybe it was the new mission, fighting ground fire instead of enemy aircraft. In a dog fight, like boxing, you're fighting an opponent, and may the best man win. But ground fire is so damned impersonal. It's iron against flesh. It's like wrasslin' a tractor instead of dozin' a bull.

"You're sure easy on an engine, Cap," Perce said. "But it's about time for an engine change and I'll bet this bird could go for another couple of hundred hours. Seems like a waste."

I was really pleased at my crew chief's remark. That was a high compliment indeed. And he was right about B6R. It did seem like a waste to junk that beautiful Rolls Royce creation, but I wasn't one to argue with the science and technology that had gone into its creation, and the restrictions those specialists had placed on its tour of duty.

Like most fighter jocks I didn't spend a lot of time thinking about the multitude of highly technical efforts that had been exerted to create our machines, and the continuing day-to-day analysis that provided the mass of information needed to successfully plan our missions. We weren't given a lot of details about how operational data was created. We were supplied with the end product, and it was precise and simple.

It might not be an oversimplification to define a fighter pilot as a "crew." He's not only a pilot, but in ground support a bombardier; a navigator on every mission, and of course a gunner and radio operator. The cockpit of the Mustang was not too roomy, so there wasn't a lot of space for "crew" paraphernalia.

Maps, charts, flight plans were reduced to a four by five inch thin aluminum plate, curved to fit your leg and held there by an elastic cord. This "clip board" was used to hold the mission slip that was filled out with briefing information for that day's assignment. Data included compass headings, distances and estimated times elapsed between check points; E.T.A.s en route, target designation, average course home from the mission area, estimated fuel consumption and even placement of the sun on the route back to home base. Radio communications info included code words and channels for Air Sea Rescue on B channel, code word Ripsaw or Roselee; Emergency landing-channel C, code word Bluefrock or Everett; Mission recall, Burlington.

The 357th's Yoxford Boys were going deep into Germany these days, and this mission was scheduled for Leipzig. Take-off was 0758 and the group set course at 0818. Our first heading was 80 degrees and 230 miles to the rendezvous with the bombers. Flying top cover, my squadron, the 363rd with the other two squadrons in the group, escorted the heavies to Southwest Berlin on a course of 112 degrees for 54 minutes, then turned almost due south for 17 minutes to Leipzig for the drop.

We had seen no enemy aircraft en route though flak was heavy in the target area. There was some broken cloud cover at the bomber level and I didn't see any B-17s going down from ground fire, but radio communications indicated some hits.

The big boys took a heading of 290 after the bomb drop, heading for Frankfurt, then turning for home. In view of the fact that there was no Luftwaffe fighter resistance, we hit the deck at a point near Dresden and turned toward home searching for targets of opportunity on the ground.

At a very low level we swept over the outskirts of Chemnitz on a heading of 290 degrees and began strafing at tree-top level anything that appeared military in nature; trucks, tanks, troops, trains, etc., etc. Our three squadrons had broken up into flights of four aircraft when we left the bombers, and my flight, D Flight, was probably the farthest north of the group. We were spread a couple of hundred yards apart, each individual choosing his own targets but still aware of the location of his partners. I was flying at about 100 feet off the ground going at somewhere between 270 or 280 indicated air speed and had just strafed and dropped my exterior wing tanks on what looked like a railroad marshalling yard at the smaller city of Weimar. The terrain beyond the city limits was rolling farmland and low wooded hills. I was roller-coasting over the swales when I entered a scene out of Dante's Inferno.

A mile or so ahead I could see the bare top of the hill, a low sprawling structure without buildings and a large open space enclosed by a high wire barricade with watch towers at intervals surrounding the compound.

As I rapidly approached, I could see the yard was packed to capacity with humanlike figures waving skeletal arms in the air over their heads. It was like a forest of small birch trees stripped bare of foliage whose bleached branches were agitated by a swirling wind. As I swept over the pitiful mass, I could see hairless heads tilted back facing me, their mouths agape in silent cries.

At first, as I continued on my course I couldn't grasp the reality of this grotesque scene that was to be engraved on my mind. Then it dawned on me. I'd seen first hand a Nazi concentration camp! Here was a living tableau of the bestiality of our enemy. I was not only revolted at the sight of this gross inhumanity, but I felt a sudden strong surge of deep, visceral anger that cried out for retribution.

Still mentally reeling over what I'd just witnessed, I was jarred out of my distraction by the arrival of one of my flight members off to my left. Soon D Flight was reformed as the other two members joined up. As soon as we crossed into friendly territory we climbed up through a low overcast and proceeded on our home course without incident. Another six-hour mission.

"There are thirty some prisoner facilities in Germany, Austria, Poland and throughout the Third Reich," said the Intelligence debriefer. "This one you saw could have been Buchenwald, one of the most infamous of them. Its prison staff has probably fled, anticipating the imminent arrival of our allied forces."

My most vivid recollections of combat seem to take the form of "stop action" snapshots; that first exploding locomotive, the blinking gunports of that ME-109 shooting at me at close range; that JU-88 that burst into flame on my first strafing run on the airdrome near Steinhuder Lake. But this was different. The Buchenwald snapshot was still life that vibrated with emotion like a Hogarth print.

Flying bomber escort and ground support fighter missions in 1944 and 1945 in the E.T.O. was to a large degree a logistical exercise. Except for the occasional dog fight, or the usual problem of evading flak, most missions involved the execution of precise operational plans; combat tactics that matched machine against machine, an impersonal duel that tested the lethal skill of the combatants. The months, even years, of training resulted in an almost automaton instantaneous reaction to each situation. When a victory was scored, it was not a kill with blood and gore. It was the disintegration of an object that was designed to eliminate you and your machine.

Today's traumatic experience changed all that. Now it was a hated enemy that manipulated that Messerschmidt 109, that Folke Wolfe 190, that ME-262. That human that was part of that malignant force that wreaked such brutal devastation upon defenseless non-combatants. Suddenly, a victory in the air was not the destruction of an enemy airplane. It was the slaying of a dragon.

Golly, I'm tired. That's about the shortest combat mission I've ever flown, but migod, it seems like a week since yesterday. I wonder what they mean by combat fatigue? When do you know if you've got it? You don't suppose it's when you go off by yourself and sit in the dark in your airplane!

Boy, we've lost some great guys lately. Three today. Even Sobol...due to go home after today. After six victories in the air he buys it on the goddamn ground. That's a helluva way to go. On his last mission. Shit!

I wish I knew if I was really good or just shot in the ass with luck.

Beats the hell out of me.

CHAPTER VIII *JANUARY 14, 1945– 56 VICTORIES*

A gaggle of geese is made up of any number of flying Canadian Honkers back home. Over Europe in 1945, a "gaggle" of Luftwaffe aircraft was anything from a flight to a squadron of enemy fighters. Today, it was a swarm of at least 80 ME-109s at 2 o'clock level, flying westerly at about 20,000 feet.

Russ Kalessa, flying Captain Browning's wing in B Flight, spotted them about the same time that Squadron Leader Bochkay called them in on the intercom frequency.

"I'd never seen so many enemy aircraft at one time," Kal recalled later. "It looked like the whole German Air Force."

The 357th, still in a group formation, was on a course heading to rendezvous and escort the bombers to the target of the day. Upon command from the group commander, they wheeled toward the approaching enemy. The three squadrons, making up the group, spread into three attack units as they turned. Gun switches were flipped into the "on" position, and the charge was initiated.

"We turned toward them immediately." I was reporting to Intelligence debriefing. "They were about 15 miles away and at the same altitude we were. It was not exactly a head-on pass, but more of a quartering attack angle. And in no time we were in the goddamndest dog fight you ever heard of."

There were fighters, theirs and ours, everywhere you looked. My job, of course, was to keep close to Carter as he attacked and fired, and to protect his tail. He quickly picked his target and clobbered the first FW-190 we closed on. Boring through the debris, we

114

went into a climbing turn, full power on, and coming out of a high turning chandelle, we tore back into the swarm. It was like diving into a cyclone's funnel. It was chillingly apparent that the biggest hazard was the possibility of a mid-air collision with one of their planes, or even with one of ours. The sky was literally swarming with wheeling and diving aircraft, extending from 20,000 feet down to 12 or 14,000 feet over an area that could be contained within six or eight hundred acres on the ground.

Carter quickly latched on to another German fighter, and this one was no amateur. He quickly pulled out all of the stops when he detected the Mustangs on his trail. He twisted, turned, snap-rolled and skidded, but Carter held on tenaciously. Finally, he sort of tumbled into a tight spiral, and we had the inside edge on him in the turns. I slid 30 or 40 feet to the outside of Carter's pursuit, intent upon keeping our path clear from another enemy sneaking up on our rear during the chase, when it happened!

I had just swiveled my head to take a quick look above and to the right, and as I looked back to adjust and maintain my position on my leader, I saw the pointed nose of an ME-109 headed right at me no less than 200 feet away off my left wing and coming fast. In a split second he roared under me, going like a bat out of hell, clearing my belly by not more than 10 feet, and was gone. How he missed ramming me broadside I'll never know.

Seconds later, like a photographic stop-action replay, I could see the silhouette of that fighter attacking me, and flashes of little lights appearing on the leading edges of his wings. Then, the delayed reaction. The sonofabitch was shooting at me! Those "lights" in his wings were muzzle flashes from his guns! At that range, he was a lousy shot!

Our dog fight seemed to go on and on. That Kraut was some pilot. Every time Carter let loose with a blast of his 50s, that bird slipped away from a fatal direct hit. A glimpse of the Swastika "Victories" painted on his canopy advertised his talent. He was damned good. But Carter was better. Finally, a long burst drew smoke and flame from the ME's nose. His canopy came off, and he hit the silk. My leader had two victories, and no remaining ammo...it was my turn.

With Carter now on my right wing covering my tail, I climbed for altitude, gaining position for our next entry into the air battle that was still going on above us. I spotted a 109 diving out of a tangle of planes slightly above us, and as he curled away I cut him off as he was making a wide leveling turn. Spotting our attack, he peeled off in a wing-over and headed almost straight down, hoping I wouldn't follow, or that he could out-dive me.

I'd been able to anticipate him a little. With full power on, I turned inside of him at the top when he did, and was able to intersect his diving course on the way down, shortening the distance between us by a hundred yards or so.

He really poured it on, as I did. I knew I was near the 400 plus mph red-line speed limit of the Mustang when I fired. The gunsight was centered, and I was right on his tail requiring no deflection lead in aiming.

The first burst struck home. A panel flew off the 109 and some smoke streamed back. The next longer burst of my 50 calibers really clobbered him and in an instant, there was a fiery burst of light and smoke as the enemy disintegrated.

I immediately tried to alter my descending course to avoid flying through the small cloud of smoke, and the debris it contained of what was left of the fragmented fighter. I tried to apply some back pressure on the stick, but at the high speed we were going, I still drilled right through the dark mass. Again, luckily, I wasn't seriously damaged. Cutting power and using the elevator trim tabs carefully, I managed to pull out and leveled off at 8,500 feet just over the cloud deck below. Finally, I could look around. There was Carter, 100 feet or so away off my right wing, looking high and low for any further potential enemy action.

The air battle was over. At the time I had no idea as to the outcome of the total engagement. I remembered hearing on the radio at the height of the fracas that another gaggle, this time FW-190s had joined the fray, and I knew we'd been outnumbered at least four to one.

No flight returned to home base that day in a formation with all four members together. The 357th Group came home in twos, threes and some by themselves. We had lost a few comrades, but during the next couple of weeks we learned the French underground had picked up those who had parachuted, and they were safe.

Colonel Dregne's 357th Fighter Group set a World War II record that day, January 14, 1945, that lasted throughout the war. The final tally, 56 confirmed victories in one mission. The 363rd Squadron accounted for 13 of the total.

That night in the Quonsets and the pilot lounges, and for many nights to come, the events of that mission were recapped a hundred or more times by those who had been there. No one person could describe the fantastic scene in its entirety. Each participant could recount his own experience, but the magnitude of the entire conflict defied description by any one individual.

"I don't remember being afraid," Lieutenant Crawford said with some amazement. "You were too damned busy to be scared. And it all started so fast you didn't have any time to anticipate what was about to happen. All of a sudden, you were in it. It was kind of like strolling through a peaceful field, and all of a sudden you were in the middle of a swarm of bees. And you knew they all had stingers."

It was a maelstrom of planes, smoke, and tracers. And speed. Everything was accelerated. Normal minutes of action were reduced to split seconds. The world outside of the cockpit went mad. You didn't plan anything. It was all instinctive reaction. You really weren't aware of flying an airplane. You became part of a projectile that lunged, parried, and thrust at an adversary that at times was almost out of focus. You literally became the machine whose only purpose was to search out and destroy another mechanism. The violent action was compressed into tremendous concentrated energy. Time lost all perspective. The combat was impersonal.

One thing I recall clearly was when the 109 I clobbered exploded, and that fight was over. But the highlight that sticks in my mind like a snapshot of a blocked kick, is those blinking flashes on the wings of that ME-109 that so barely missed lighting me up.

"I saw the son-of-a-bitch, I tell you! It was a Mustang, and he shot Browning in his chute!" Captain Harry Jones, Leader of the 362nd Fighter Squadron's B Flight, was not prone to make extravagant statements. Jones had flown his 47th mission that day, and had boosted his confirmed victories to nine in the air. He was an experienced combat veteran, and he had thought he knew how the game was being played.

"I'd heard they were doing that," he continued, "but I couldn't believe my eyes...I saw him take hits earlier from a 109 that got on his tail while he was pumping lead into another...he smoked and I saw him jettison his canopy."

Lieutenant Avery, Jones' wingman, confirmed his leader's account. "Cap is right. That's exactly what happened, and we circled around to see if he got clear all right."

Jones nodded and continued. "We were at about 12,000 feet, just west of Stuttgart, when Brownie's bird gave out. I figured he would free-fall, maybe wait to pull the ripcord until he reached the overcast at about 8,000 feet. I was real surprised to see his chute open so fast...he only fell free about a couple of thousand feet." Harry Jones paused, as if the scene was being rerun in slow motion in his mind. "We followed him down in a big arc spiral kind of, and suddenly here comes this lone P-51 out of nowhere, spittin' tracers and clobbering him in his chute..."

The witness paused, his eyes staring out over the heads of his audience. Then in a low voice, more as if he was thinking out loud, "We never got off a burst...before we could get in range, he disappeared into the overcast...the Kraut 51 was gone...and so was Browning."

The Ready Room of the 362nd, like other squadrons after a mission, usually buzzed with a dozen pilots all talking at once, giving their account of their part in the day's events. This debriefing session was different...the room was deathly silent. All eyes were trained on Captain Jones who stood facing them, standing rigid before the huge map of Europe on the wall behind him. This last disclosure about the mysterious Mustang was met with stunned disbelief.

"What color was its tail and spinner?" A low, intense voice, hoarse with emotion came from the rear of the room. Major Don Bochkay, squadron leader of the 363rd had joined the others and had been listening to Jones' report. "What about identification letters...numbers...anything?" he demanded.

Harry Jones looked at Bochkay sadly. He knew "Bock" and Browning had been best buddies. He knew how this news was tearing at him. "Sorry, Major. That '51 was just camouflaged green and gray all over...no color on the tail or spinner. No numbers or letters I could see. He just made that one pass, a real long burst of the 50s...then he rolled over and split-essed into the cloud cover about 1,200 or 1,300 feet below. It was over in 15 seconds."

CHAPTER IX *AN EYE FOR AN EYE*

I stepped out of the smoke-filled shack into rare blinding sunshine. My eyes, streaming in the brilliant glare, were quickly shaded as I covered them with my Raband sun glasses. I was still stunned by the account we had just witnessed. We had heard reports of the enemy shooting our pilots in their chutes, I recalled...nothing official, but still too frequent to be just rumors. Now it was confirmed!

Early in the history of aviation there had been a universal kinship among pilots of all nationalities. When Lindy made his heroic solo leap across the Atlantic, pilots everywhere rejoiced and hailed him. During World War I, in spite of the ferocious combat being waged by their comrades on the ground, pilots on both sides maintained a sort of "code of the skies." Airmen, universally, admired the feats of the pursuit pilots, as they were then known, flying "kites" made of "paper and bamboo" called Spads and Fokkers. They marveled at the exploits of the "Red Baron," Richover, and Eddie Rickenbacker alike. The two aerial forces met on the skies over France and Germany much like knights jousting during the Crusades. And, when defeated over enemy turf, if the pilot survived the return to earth, he was toasted, fed, wined and entertained by his "captors" as "one of them." This, that had to some degree started out more or less honoring the old traditions, was now different. The knightly charger had become a bestial war horse.

"That Mustang." I had heard Intelligence reports a few weeks earlier that a P-51 had been landed by a dying pilot on an Autobahn in enemy territory. An L-5 liaison-plane pilot, flying reconnaissance for Patton's Third Army had witnessed the landing, and reported the pilot had not emerged from the craft, and that there had been no sign of an explosion or fire. The P-51 pilot had obviously expired before he could destroy his ship.

"They got it, all right," I thought. "And any trained fighter pilot could fly it with no sweat. Hell, there are dozens of Luftwaffe jocks that could fly it. And they'd found one who was also an assassin!"

Head up now, I strode off through the steaming late afternoon light toward the Quonset quarters area.

"Tomorrow is another day. Yessir. Tomorrow is a brand new ballgame."

Dear Lolly,

Just a short note to tell you that Browning bought it yesterday. I'm still having a little trouble believing it, but it happened for sure. Seems like yesterday when he and I were playing Snooker.

Thought you might want to call his folks in Flora, Illinois. They ought to be in the book. The Army will have notified them by the time you get this. Tell them that I'll see to it that all of his personal stuff gets home to them. I'll sure go and see them when this is all over.

You know I'm not going to "turn the other cheek" as the Good Book says.

                    Love,
                    Alan

Though it was tied down, the Mustang quivered and rocked with each gust of wind. The driving pellets of rain, propelled like buckshot, beat a tattoo on the skin of the silent resting charger. This steed was more than just a metal instrument of war. It was damn near flesh and blood. It roared when it was stressed to the edge of its limits. It purred when it was tuned in flight to its best settings. Even now, sitting silent in the darkness, it seemed merely dozing, trembling a little as if dreaming of tomorrow's test that was sure to come.

Sitting in the cockpit I wasn't really thinking. A mental numbness seemed to have enveloped me. I wasn't exactly aware of how I came to be there. In some way the storm raging outside the canopy was perfectly appropriate. Though my clothes were soaking wet, I felt warm and secure. There was nothing in this cramped, familiar space that could harm me, and no outside threat to disturb this refuge that, for now, was calm and peaceful.

Damn. There's that turned-to-stone feeling again. I told Don about that. I feel almost detached from my body. I know I could lift my feet if I really wanted to. But I just don't want to. To hell with it. It goes away. It always does.

Hello Earlduke. Hello Earlduke. This is Cement 79. Has Browning called in? He's overdue, and...

Sorry, Tilly. He'd think I'd gone completely over the edge if I did that. I know better. The son of a bitch is gone. And I gotta get used to it.

How the hell are you supposed to get used to it? I've tried to keep a little distance from my guys. It's sure tough to do when your life depends on them, and theirs on you. But goddamn, you couldn't function when you were grieving all the time.

Just listen to the rain. It's different than it sounds in the barn. This rain has a sad sound. And the wind moaning away isn't any help. It sure doesn't stop for long over here. It didn't stop even for Wilmot's funeral. Thank God, Brownie won't have to go through that! Standing at attention in a gale while Chappie does his thing. And Taps! I hate a goddamn bugle. I never want to hear Taps again. Browning said the same thing. Well, buddy. You went out fast the way we all say we want to.

Well, not quite the way we want it. You sure didn't get clobbered in a fair fight. No. That Nazi bastard executed you when you couldn't fight back. It's that simple.

Maybe it is that *simple*. What the hell do you think this is? A Golden Gloves boxing match? Where's the referee? Where is the Marquis of Queensbury? There isn't anyone, you idiot! Those Krauts know how to play this game, and you'd better start playing by their rules.

I think I've finally figured it out. I've finally got it. I don't catch on too fast. I even think the coach will understand.

God, I'm tired.

The shadowy form appeared as he rolled back the canopy of the parked aircraft, scissored out onto the wing and carefully inched down the greasy surface to the ground. He stood there a few seconds, patted the side of the Mustang, and stopped to haul out the bike he had slid under the wing earlier. Pushing the bike across the glistening, metal Pierce planking of the hardstand, he made his way to the nearby taxi way. Mounting carefully, he headed down the concrete perimeter track to the access road, up the slight rise that led to the headquarters area and the B.O.Q. Quonset huts not visible in the wet darkness.

The rider wasn't challenged as he passed the dimly lit sentry box that guarded the entrance to the flight line. Corporal Malachi had been briefed earlier about the presence on the field of the cyclist by the A.P. he had relieved at midnight. "Yeah, he's an officer alright. He was wearing a 50-mission-crush billed cap with the gold eagle, and an A-2 leather jacket that had the 363rd's emblem painted on the back. He didn't act drunk. He was slow but steady on his bike in spite of the damn wind and rain. I called it in, but Sarge said it was O.K. Just to let him know if he didn't come out. No doubt he was a jock. No ground-pounder is going to be out in this crap when he could be in the sack."

Well, "the jock" had come out. The corporal strained his eyes trying to pick up a sign of movement across the almost impenetrable darkness of the blacked-out air base, and finally saw his man turning towards the Quonset area as he passed under the hooded street light that marked the base headquarters.

The guard turned to crank his field phone that connected with his command center and was relieved to learn that he could wrap up this incident that was so rare during what was usually a really dull, monotonous routine.

"Hey Sarge. This is Malachi, Post 3. The bike jockey just pedaled his ass home...No, I didn't talk to him, he went right on by and didn't even look at me...Boy, some of these pilots are strange ducks, aren't they...Hey, that's right. Only a duck would be out on a night like this."

The sound of a motorcycle engine overhead, missing badly, coughing and sputtering, broke the pre-dawn silence of the dripping East Anglia countryside. Four men in a jeep, swathed in slickers, and wearing billed caps covered with plastic dish covers, looked up into the leaden overcast and speculated where that "stovepipe" loaded with destruction would finally crash. Leiston Airdrome, home base of the 357th Fighter Group, U.S. Army Air Corps, was directly in the path of Buzz Bomb Alley, the route taken by the V-2 flying bombs that had been launched moments before across the English Channel in German-occupied territory. Their destination, London, to wreck terrible havoc on that still slumbering, helpless city.

"One of these nights, some Kraut technician is going to screw up the timing and one of those babies is going to wake us up," I said. "Isn't that a gutless thing to do? Not even a pilot in the damned thing. Just a bucket of bolts, bailing wire and a guidance system. And, the payload! Soon a bunch of poor Limeys are going to get clobbered while still in their sacks."

The jeep, splashing through sopping, pitted tarmac careened on its way to the officers' mess hall like a landing craft hitting the beach. The driver, like the other passengers, was a fighter pilot, and he drove any land-locked vehicle with great impatience. He could never quite adjust from 300 mph fighter air speed to the snail pace of any land vehicle. It was like stepping off a fast escalator and learning to walk again. It was not surprising that there were nearly as many casualties caused by jeep and bicycle crashes as were suffered in combat. A pilot, full of gin and bitters, biking home in the black-out from the local pub, was destined for the dispensary. Busted kneecaps and elbows gained in this fashion didn't rate a Purple Heart.

But, this jeep jockey, careening through the drizzling darkness, delivered his passengers safely, though shaken, to the Quonset hut that loomed like a huge wet barrel lying on its side in the sodden mud of England.

"I don't think we'll go today," said Wingman Crawford hopefully. "I just saw a duck, walking."

Entering the mess hall with my companions I ignored Crawford's use of what was a well-worn expression to describe lousy weather, and blew my nose with gusto. "We'll get a mission alright, and it won't be a milk run." I peeled off my shiny, olive-colored raincoat like a snake shedding its skin, and hung it with my "50 mission-crush" officer's cap on the rack with others of its kind.

I was in a foul mood. "I can just see those ground pounders down at Cambridge right now," I continued, "with their fat bellies full of real eggs and real milk, and punching out the latest Sting from Wing on the teletype."

We joined the silent line of other pilots chowing up. The steam table bins were filled with the usual: powdered eggs, soggy toast, limp bacon, and hash browns that looked like dried mud. Beverages included powdered milk, grainy and chalky, some kind of fruit punch, and coffee that came from Brazil in the hold of an old oil tanker.

"Gee whiz! Isn't this great cuisine?" said 2nd Lieutenant Black sarcastically. "Everyone told me what great chow the 357th had. They said the mess sergeant had his own restaurant in Manhattan." "That's right," responded Crawford. "His chili was supposed to cure ulcers. It would even cure a cough. Eat one bowl and you didn't dare cough."

Element Leader Taylor hadn't spoken a word since leaving the B.O.Q. He was a night person he often said, and nothing should happen before noon. Now he was spurred to speech. "The only thing worse than this damned slop is the quality of humor in this flight," he muttered. "How come we're so lucky to have two comics to entertain us, Ab? I should have stood in bed."

I was still engrossed in my jaundiced vision of the mission planners at work in the ivory towers of wing headquarters, and ignored the chaffing of my crew. "Do you guys remember that Plans Room at Wing? Leather Chairs, green drapes and a table like a football field? Good Lord, you could land a Piper L-5 on it. And, that map! Little colored pins. The 357th is pink for Christ's sake! That's what we are—a little pink pin! And they're probably going to stick it to us again, those chair-borne bastards!"

My "team" was silent during my intense outburst. Such vehemence, though subdued, was totally unlike me. They knew me only as a calm, well-disciplined officer, as well as a dedicated "company man." I would grouse like anyone else about food, leave, weather, but never a word disloyal to my superiors. I went by the written, and unwritten book.

The team studiously continued eating their rapidly cooling breakfast. I couldn't seem to get out of this morose funk. I'd been this way since yesterday's mission over Stuttgart when Browning "bought it." Browning, major, ace twice over, and group operations officer, was one of the outfit's hottest pilots. Where others were damned good, he was really outstanding. He could do things with a P-51 that lesser jockeys knew were impossible. And no Luftwaffe fighter had ever come close to shooting him down. Until yesterday.

The disastrous defeat Field Marshal Goering's Luftwaffe had suffered on January 15, may have been the final coup de grace the 8th Air Force had been looking for. At any rate, today's mission to Munich had been uneventful, as far as any fighter opposition was concerned. There had been plenty of flak and heavy ground fire when they'd strafed the airdrome at Neubiberg just south of the old Bavarian capital. After the last bombing run was completed, the 363rd F.S. had descended from their low-cover escort position, and headed south toward the distant Alps. Dropping to tree-top level, the squadron roared down the placid surface of the Worm Lake, echelonned right, and broke into two-ship elements as they made a wide sweeping turn to the heading of 45 degrees, that in seconds would bring the Luftwaffe air base under their blazing 50 calibers.

I had performed well this day with seasoned proficiency. Flying Bochkay's wing had become almost routine. I felt it was a real compliment for him to pick me. Routine that is, as far as flying technique was concerned. I could now choreograph my movements to coincide perfectly to any maneuver he might execute. And, I did do it damn well.

The ground attack on the aerodrome completed, I applied power as my leader took up a climbing heading of 300 degrees for home. Knowing this course was somewhat south of the average course home, I knew "Bock" was avoiding any risk of flying too low over any elements of Patton's Third Army. Only last week we'd been fired upon by some "friendly" ground troops who were too weary to be greatly concerned about careful aircraft identification.

Levelling off at 12,000 feet, still holding a westerly heading, we proceeded past Augsburg, Ulm, and in the distance, could cross the Rhine near Strasbourg. Fuel was a consideration, but we still had enough to easily reach England.

Suddenly, Bock jerked his thumb toward me, and broke sharply to his right. Sliding under my leader, I took up my turning position on the opposite side of the still banking lead Mustang. I looked intently, swiftly scanning the sky, high and low, trying to determine what interested my commander.

"What in hell does he see?" I wondered. I was one wingman who didn't ask a lot of questions while in flight. Major Bochkay, never one to break radio silence unnecessarily, had been even less communicative lately. As he levelled in flight and turned back to our original heading, he still gave no indication of what he'd spotted that was so interesting.

Turning north over Strasbourg, we proceeded up the Rhine River towards Mannheim and Wiesbaden. Once, far off, a few moving specks at an altitude slightly higher than ours, had appeared going eastward. It may have been a small gaggle of German fighters going in that direction, but too far to do anything about. Our two Mustangs droned on in a routine, almost dull fashion.

There was something different about Bock's technique today. Any flight leader, mission completed and homeward bound, normally would relax somewhat, do the navigating, watch for ground check points, and leave sky surveillance up to his ever alert wingman. Not "Bock." Not today...His head turned constantly, swiveling from point to point, right to left, and back again...searching the horizon...scanning high and low, as if expecting a surprise attack at any moment.

I had noticed this new behavior earlier, soon after we'd left Munich, and started home. There was nothing fearful in Bochkay's attitude or action. It was just different. And vaguely ominous.

My headphones suddenly crackled into life. "Bogie...2:00 o'clock...look alive," "Bock" snapped, and immediately increased power to gain an anticipated need for altitude advantage.

"Holy cow, he's spotted one," I thought, suddenly realizing that he had not been scanning the skies defensively....

"He'd been hunting!"

The "Bogie" quickly became a "Bandit," a confirmed enemy aircraft. It was an ME-262, one of the relatively new jet fighters the Germans had developed too late. This one, obviously saving fuel, was in a slightly nose-down attitude, and descending to the southeast. The Nazi pilot hadn't spotted us diving out of the afternoon sun, and continued his power glide unaware of our now-launched attack.

Bock clobbered him on the initial pass. Covering the action, I saw the enemy jet belch black smoke, as the pilot applied power too late when he realized he was under attack. The first burst from Bock's six 50 calibers hit the target full broadside. Panels tore off the fuselage as the intense gunfire ripped along the nose and back to the tail section. Part of the horizontal stabilizer disintegrated, and as smoke and fire began to erupt from the engine section, the canopy flew off...Seconds later, the ME-262 pilot hit the silk.

"He got him...he got him!" "One burst, and he clobbered hell out of him!"

Bock roared under the destroyed fighter plane, and pulled up in a high-speed wing-over as he reversed course and came back in a steep dive on the track of the falling Nazi pilot. I had closed and crossed over my leader, and followed suit. Now, line abreast with him, a scant 30 feet off his wing on the right, our two roaring Mustangs thundered downward on the trail of the escaping enemy.

Long seconds passed before either of us saw the falling speck plummeting toward a scattered cloud cover some 5,000 feet below. Suddenly, a parasol burst, and the chute billowed wide. There was the target!

Bock, coming in at a steep 45-degree angle, guns blazing, shredded the chute, and set the dangling doll attached to it dancing like a puppet on strings. I followed, acting in automated unison, duplicating my leader's ferocious execution.

It was many moments later before the realization of what had happened fully came home. I felt no thrill of victory, no exultation. Likewise, I also felt no overpowering sensations of guilt or remorse. If anything, the whole incident had a rather abstract quality. There was nothing really personal about it. I'd been trained to shoot moving targets. I'd been disciplined to follow my leader. Anywhere. And the final rationalization, "Why shoot down a goddamn enemy airplane, and have the pilot live to shoot you down tomorrow?" And, of course, there was Browning.

GUN CAMERA. A gun camera is mounted in the leading edge of the left wing, and is accessible for loading and adjustment from the left wheel well. A small door covers the camera's aperture in the wing; this door remains open in flight, but is closed by a mechanical linkage when the landing gear is extended, thus protecting the lens from blown sand or pebbles when the airplane is on the ground. Guns and camera are controlled by a three-position switch on the front switch panel; this switch also turns on the lamp in the optical sight. With the switch flicked up to GUNS, CAMERA 7 SIGHT, when the guns fire, the camera operates when you press the trigger on the stick.

We were seven minutes to landfall at 50 feet over the Channel, flying almost directly into the setting winter sun, when I thought about the gun camera. The gun camera; that on 8mm film recorded every hit scored by those six 50-calibre guns. Every foot of that film was processed and viewed by the photo lab crew, and then, if any action had taken place, was again monitored and analyzed by the Intelligence guys. "They all would see it. What would they think? After all, they weren't combat types. It wasn't as if other jocks would see it—even the C.O. He had 12 victories. He knew what the score was. But ground-pounders! Desk jockeys! Guys who'd never been there. They didn't know what it was like!"

After landing, cutting power on the big Merlin engine, I came to rest in a hardstand next to Major Bochkay's spot, where my squadron commander was already climbing out of his cockpit. I quickly unsnapped and leaped to the ground.

Bochkay stood, helmet off, parachute draped over his shoulder, waiting near a jeep standing by to ferry us to the Squadron Ready Room. He stared at me as I approached. He was expressionless, no emotion showing on his drawn, bleak Irish face.

"Major," I said in a low anxious voice as I drew near, "the film! The gun camera. It's all there. On film!"

Major Donald Bochkay, Commander of the 363rd Fighter Squadron, 357th Fighter Group, 8th Air Force, USAF, stated flatly, "That's the way it is," and turned away, slamming his parachute in the back seat of the muttering jeep. It had started to rain.

CHAPTER X D-DAY IN PICCADILLY CIRCUS

"You can mix rye whiskey with Coke, club soda, orange or to-mato juice, or coffee, tea or milk, and it still will taste like 100 oc-tane." I was not happy with my liquor ration. A 48-hour pass to London required certain provisions that were more palatable and marketable than a quart of rye whiskey. Granted, there were some barkeeps that would trade a quart of Johnny Walker Red Label scotch for two bottles of rye, but only because they could water down the rye, and still get a trace of booze flavor in a "bourbon and soda" order.

I continued my interrogation of Casey, my travelling compan-ion on this coveted non-combat mission to the English metropolis. "What's this? One bottle of rye and one bottle of scotch for each of us; eight Hershey bars, four apiece; two cartons of Domino ciga-rettes, and two cartons of Camels. Well, my Camels stay home. Anyone I'd meet, raised on a diet of Players, cannot appreciate these babies."

This ritual was played out daily all over the U.K. as combat crews were released from flying duty to play in the "sand boxes" so plentiful in London Town. This vast city might as well have been the size of three or four football fields which could contain Piccadilly Circus, the core of the city's night life. Nighttime, and daytime too for that matter, the area was crammed with enlisted and officer personnel living it up. Restaurants, theatres, pubs, bars and hotels were filled with consumers. All bent on having a brief good time while their wartime paused a moment.

128

"What's the tab, mate?" Casey asked the cab driver who delivered us to Piccadilly Circus from Victoria Railroad Station. "Eight shillings, Guvner," he replied. The cabbie, smiling as he pocketed the 10 shilling note the American had given him, tugged at the bill of his cap and pulled way with a "'ave a pint for me, gentlemen, and good 'unting."

"Good chap," said Casey, mimicking his British friends. "We jolly well will have some good hunting, old boy. Two-legged game of course. Also some good scotch, and we might even find a piece of beef that didn't come off a horse." Sunday night in Soho, the date was May 6, 1945.

Monday, May 7, 1945, was a miserable day. Oh, the sun was shining and birds flying, and green grass and flowers flourished in Hyde Park. But from where Casey and I saw it, through blood shot, swollen eyes, it was a far different vista. We had "jolly well" tied one on. Neither of us had been near the windows of our hotel rooms overlooking the square, where a midday sun sent dazzling rays upon the cobblestones that, had they been less impregnable, would have long ago dissolved during the long months of England's winters. As Mr. Lewis Carroll put it, it was a "fraptious day" outside.

The Boar's Head was a pub at night. During daylight hours it catered to a few select customers as a café. I had been introduced and vouched for by Squadron Leader Bochkay to the owners Harry Orwell and his cockney wife, Pam. 'Array was a first rate bartender, but Pamela was an ingenious cook. Her meat loaf was edible! What she could do with this concoction, consisting as it did, of a minute portion of real meat and the balance made up of cereal, ground vegetables and whatever else was handy, was something rather remarkable. Unlike other recipes found throughout the city, hers did not contain sawdust!

The British had a saying about the Yanks who were stationed everywhere throughout the United Kingdom. "They're over-paid, over-sexed, and over here." The British Armed Forces said it with some bitterness due to the great difference in pay, and the attraction the Yanks held for the English girls. Civilians, who relied on the visitors for a good portion of their trade, said it to each other, but in good humor. It was rarely pointed directly to a G.I.

There's little doubt the Americans did not always behave in a manner that was very endearing to their hosts. They often drank too much, they spent their money too freely, and were not always appreciative of the shortages that severely limited the availability of foodstuffs. Concerned with their own involvement in the war, they were generally not sufficiently impressed with the ordeal these long-suffering people had endured for so long. There were some Yanks who had been in London during a Blitz raid, and had joined the locals in the air raid shelters until the "all clear" sounded. They quickly gained a new respect for the courage and fortitude these English of all classes could summon in adversity. "Their finest hour" extended into years.

Pamela (Starke) Orwell, like many of her West End "sisters," was a good deal more than just a good cook. She was a born and bred Londoner, and had been through the Blitz from its beginning some four years before. When Hermann Goering ordered the Luftwaffe to unleash the bombardment of London with incendiary bombs in the hope of destroying with fire the morale of the citizenry of the town of seven million souls, Pam joined the fight.

The home guard that had been concerned with high explosive destruction bombs, now moved from the bomb craters, blackouts and shelters to the roof tops. Volunteer "roof spotters" were orga-nized by the National Fire Service, and they spent their nights on London's rooftops extinguishing fires caused by the nightly raids. The "Jim Crows," as Pam and her comrades were called, fought fires through a period that saw as many as 70,000 incendiary bombs dropped in a month. With each dawn, the city would be enshrouded with smoke, and marked in all directions by the light of hundreds of fires still burning.

It was during this time that Pam met ex-Lance Corporal Harry Orwell, a recently released veteran of the campaigns in North Africa where he served with General Montgomery, and where he lost his left leg below the knee while fighting a skirmish with troops of Rommel's desert forces. His handicap did not deter Harry Orwell for long. He soon put his war-gained expertise to work, and became a member of the U.X.B., the Unexploded Bomb squads. The German bombers now were dropping large numbers of delayed-action bombs on the city, and the unknown time set for their detonation caused great anxiety among the general populace as well as considerable damage to airfields, factories, and main thoroughfares. The latent bombs had to be dug out and exploded or defused. The volunteers playing this deadly game sometimes neutralized successfully 20 or 30 attempts before their luck ran out. Harry Orwell had scored 32 "victories" when the ordeal ended.

During this time Harry and Pam shared the same address with a few hundred other occupants.

c/o Tunnel Shelter, Ramsgate, London.

They, and the others literally lived underground for a very long period. The two "volunteers" met at odd moments when Pam was not extinguishing fires at night, and Harry had a relief from his daytime U.X.B. bomb duties. But, like so many couples in wartime, they found time for courtship, and eventually wed.

"This'll be over someday Luv," Pam would say. "And, if the Boche don't bomb it to 'ell, maybe the Old Man's pub will find room for us. You'll be surprised 'ow good I can cook on a real stove, and I know you've 'ad a lot of experience with ale and spirits. You'd look well *behind* a bar for a change."

"Air Rescue Service, 12:00 o'clock level," said Casey, as we, two casualties of the "Battle of Piccadilly," trudged toward the refuge offered by our favorite tavern. I had not failed to bring my Musette bag that contained not only my pass rations, but a few items that had been obtained by a Midnight Requisition from the 357th Group mess hall supplies.

"Ah luv, but ain't you a sight!" said Pamela, as she greeted us as we stood rather sheepishly in her doorway. "Well, get yourselves in 'ere—and shut the door. It ain't Summer yet, Luv. Yer lettin all my 'eat out, and my coal ration is running low. Doff yer reefers and grab a seat. I'll fix you a toddy before yer bleed to death." With that, she turned into the small galley and reappeared with a steaming tea kettle.

"You may well save our lives, Darlin'," I said. "I don't know what we'd do without you." With that, I lifted the Musette bag, placed it on the bar and started to unload my swag. "Let's see," I said. "These powdered eggs were laid last year in the State of Idaho. This powdered milk is from a prize-winning Jersey cow named Elsie who lives in Maine. Now you may think this Spam is ordinary Spam. But, no, it's made from an old recipe handed down from my grandmother. And the peanut butter is peanut butter."

Both Case and I grinned with delight at the wide-eyed reception these remarks and the sight of the food obtained from their hostess.

"Luv a duck, you are a smasher ain't yer?" whispered the obviously impressed lady. "Here, drink this, you pirates," she said, putting a steaming toddy in front of each of them. "I'll fix you the best breakfast you've ever 'ad, what with all these victuals you've brought." And she did. Two hours later, fortified by Pam's cooking and a couple more toddies, we were now revived airmen and emerged into a late afternoon lit by a setting sun. Surprisingly, the weather had improved considerably, or at least our tolerance for bright, broad daylight had.

"How in hell can you make an omelet with powdered eggs?" said Casey. "Migod. If she was a Mess Sergeant, I'd sign up for life."

———————————

We had arrived at the Blue Boar pub somewhat the worse for wear. When we left, thanks to the ministrations rendered by Pam Orwell, if not new men, we were at least much improved. It really was a nice day.

The pub was located on a side street a few blocks from Piccadilly Circus, and as we turned toward that square, we paused and looked at each other. Something was different. Something was up!

Now we became aware of a muffled roar that seemed to be coming from a few blocks away. Our pace quickened as we now hurried toward its source. A brief street brawl between Yanks and "Limeys" was not uncommon, but there were no sounds of police klaxons or alarms. This was a new sound.

As we rounded a corner into a broader thoroughfare, we found people running toward the square.

"Hey, what's up?" Casey shouted at them. "What's happening?"

A wild-eyed Londoner, waving his cap in one hand and his umbrella in the other, screamed as he raced by. "It's over, Yank! The bastards surrendered! It's all over!"

We stood stock still, as if in shock. Finally, we eased out of the swirling torrent into the shelter of a tobacco shop doorway. The moving crowd, gaining in numbers, continued to stream past. Some of the older ones paused in their efforts to keep up, and stood leaning against a wall, some with tears streaming down their cheeks. The younger ones, mostly girls and teenage lads, were laughing and screaming as they raced to the celebration, and away from the war.

Neither of us had spoken to the other since the news had finally sunk in. We had stood rather dazedly, staring at the scene before us. Finally, we faced each other and solemnly shook hands.

"Well, we did it," Casey said. "By god, we all did it."

"Yeah," I responded, "we sure as hell did and I do mean We."
"But," I continued, "it's funny, I don't feel like celebrating. I haven't been in two years, but suddenly I feel like going to church."

"I know what you mean," said Casey. "But I have never seen one in this part of town. Guess we might as well follow the crowd. The Circus must be packed by now. We shouldn't miss it, I guess."

Realistically, the military extended all liberty and leaves for varying lengths of time. They knew exhaustion would within hours overtake the revelers, and they would return to their bases to recuperate.

We lasted another 24 hours in the wildest city we'd ever experienced. As we later told our less fortunate comrades who'd been on duty call at the 357th, "You couldn't *buy* a drink anywhere in town. Every bar and pub just gave it away. They never stopped thanking us for helpin' out. The funny thing is, we both kind of lost our appetite for booze. Funny thing."

EPILOGUE

After V E Day, the 357th Fighter Group still maintained combat readiness. After a brief period of down-time while things kind of settled a bit, and the celebrations died down, the Group continued to fly daily. After all, there was still a war going on in the Pacific. And this outfit expected to get into it.

The first step in "getting into it" occurred some weeks later when the Group moved to Munich, Germany as part of the Army of Occupation, and prepared to move east across Asia to the Japanese Theatre. It never happened. President Harry Truman and the A Bomb finished that one.

I was a fighter pilot without a war, and holder of a few awards and decorations. Like my fellow pilots of the 357th Group, I learned upon being discharged from the Air Corps, and back in the stateside labor pool, that fighter jocks were not in big demand as civilian employees. The commercial airlines accepted applications from four-engine aircraft pilots, with 2,500 hours flying time, 500 hours of which had to be in the bomber's left seat as First Pilot. There was only one seat in a Mustang!

There have been many accounts written about the difficulties experienced by combat personnel in making the transition from military service to civilian life. World War II veterans did return as victors, and were welcomed with parades and celebrations. They were lucky. This was the last war after which American fighting men came home as heroes.